Help is on the Way:

An Exploration of the Road to Ruin

For The Sick and The Tired

Introduction

Never concern yourself about anything that lies beyond your control. If it is not up to you, do not worry about it. Of course, this is *far* easier said than done, but this little bit of cognitive restructuring will spare you an enormous amount of needless psychological and emotional distress. The dysfunctional belief that the world *must* be or *should* be some way other than the way that it *is*, nearly always results in frustration, anxiety, and despair. Do not *expect* the world to conform to your pre-reflective desires or expectations. The world *owes* you *nothing*. Remember that. Learn to adopt the posture of *rational indifference* about all of those things that you cannot change about the world or about yourself. Do not, as it were, insist upon being "taller than you are," or upon inhabiting a world that functions in accordance with your whims. Learn to make your desires and expectations conform to the world as it is, and to the future as it unfolds. If you find the world dissatisfying, then the *world* is *not* the problem. The world was here long before *you* showed up. The world is large and you are small. *Respect* that.

Focus your energies on the facets of yourself that you *can* change, and note how much less frequently you find that you are troubled or dissatisfied. The Stoics, the Cynics, and the Buddhists (not to mention practitioners of other ancient wisdom traditions) have understood and taught this fundamental lesson for thousands of years. Its intuitive plausibility is fairly straightforward. If you encounter some condition about which you can do *nothing* (and you *will* encounter *many* such conditions), then getting upset and overwrought about the things you cannot control is just begging for lots of unpleasantness in your emotional and psychological states. You will gain *nothing* from steeping in constant anxiety and worry. Your body will suffer along with your mind, and you will find it much more difficult to sleep, digest food, and relax your muscles. Nothing saps your energy like worrying your way through every waking moment. You do not *have* to live with this kind of relentless, debilitating anxiety. You *can* manage your mental states much more effectively than that. The author of this book has spent decades struggling against anxiety, and much of that time was, regrettably, *wasted* on unenlightened and poorly conceived efforts.

Luckily, the author also stumbled across a few sources that proved to be genuinely useful. This book is a collection of several months of written meditations concerning the conditions over which the author has no control, the few phenomena that author *can* control, and sporadic ruminations about the author's bouts of confusion, alienation, and a gradual, meandering progress toward something vaguely like equanimity (or at least something vaguely *less* like despair).

You are invited to tag along on the author's stumbling travels through the inner realm of consciousness. Perhaps you will recognize some of the awkwardness and the uncertainty through which the author bumbles. We *are* all merely humans, after all. Everyone struggles. Hopefully, you will make progress over time. Of course, there are no guarantees that you will make the kind of progress for which you may hope. There are, in fact, no guarantees about *anything*. There is only this moment, right now. Here you are. Here is a book. Only *you* can decide what *you* want to do with it. So, what is it going to be? Keep reading and perhaps some answers will emerge from within you. *You* get to decide what to do with whatever you find as you explore the contents of your own mind. No one else can get inside there. Help is *not* on the way where *your* mental states are concerned. Your consciousness is *yours* to control and *yours* to observe. It is yours to *attempt* to master. Have you taken the time and made the effort to get to know yourself from the inside out? If not, then you are missing out on some important experience. The author of this book encourages you to root around

and see what you may have
missed. The exploration is
bound to be worth the effort,
is it not?

Muddled Observations

February 24, 2021

You talk to yourself a lot. As far as you can tell, just about everybody else does also. Perhaps you might benefit from writing some of your thoughts down in a journal. If nothing else, it may at least relieve the burden of hauling all of these ideas and observations around with you everywhere you go. It feels like these thoughts take up a lot of space that could be used for better purposes. Try getting part of this stuff out of your head and storing it in some receptacle in the outside world. Perhaps the cognitive congestion that you often experience will abate somewhat if you provide a means of exit for some of the detritus rattling around inside your head. Who knows, maybe other people might recognize some commonality with your experiences and your various forms of confusion. You cannot be the *only* one who so frequently has no idea what the hell is happening or why it is so difficult to figure out what, if anything, you are supposed to be doing about any of it. Surely, others are baffled as well, right? You cannot be the only person on the planet who no longer recognizes the place in which you find yourself, or the people by whom you are surrounded. When did everything get turned upside down and inside out? Did you sleep through some massive and sudden sociocultural shift? It sure feels that way. This world that sprawls out all around you becomes more alien with each passing year. Indeed, it often seems to become stranger by the *day*. You keep encountering people who say the most ludicrous things imaginable, and they assert their bizarre delusions as if they are incontrovertible fact. They may as well be speaking some language that you have never heard before. All of that is, in the final analysis, neither good nor bad. It is all just *weird*. A *lot* of things are like that. Let the emotional "bleeders" carp and moan to their hearts' content. Keep a reasonable distance. What *else* can you do about these lunatics? Do not rely upon other people for maintaining your serenity and peace of mind. The masses are no foundation for stability or sanity. Avoid crowds like the plague (that they *are*).

February 25, 2021

You see and hear things that would have been utterly unthinkable just a decade ago (or less). *Very* few of the changes to the social fabric seem to be for the better, and very few of these changes make you more sanguine about the future of this nation and its culture. While technology advances by quantum leaps and bounds, it seems that humanity becomes ever more decadent, depraved, and distanced from reality. It looks like people now inhabit a world for which they are entirely unprepared and largely ill-suited. The only people who act as if they know what they are doing are the ones who maniacally seek power over others. Once they *attain* the power they seek, they immediately set about destroying anything that was once noble, wholesome, or admirable. How did *you* let this happen? How did *everyone* let this happen? Think on it a bit. Do *not* expect your thinking to change anything about the world as it now stands. These are *strange* days. The future looks to be even stranger still. Observe, report, and ponder all you like. Spill your thoughts onto a page or a screen to your heart's content. Share your observations and musings with those who wish to read them. Think of this as a form of therapy if you like. It might even prove therapeutic for some of those who read what you write. Of course, it might *not*. There is, you can only suppose, but *one* reliable way to find out. Keep "talking" to yourself here on these pages. See if it helps. See if anyone cares about what you write. What, after all, is the *worst* that can happen? It is not that much different, in *this* case, from that *best* that can happen, is it? Reason your way through to the point that you are confident you are thinking for *yourself* as opposed to thinking in accordance with expectations imposed by others. At some stage of the "creative" process, you will have time for a sandwich, perhaps. Hopefully, you will achieve something more than that, but you probably should not *count* on doing so.

February 26, 2021

The first thing you noticed this morning was the ache in the center of your lower back as you rolled over to grab your morning pills. This way of waking up has become *very* familiar to you. Both components of this experience are worth noting. Your back hurts more and more frequently these days (as well as more intensely most days), and you have to take pills every day, or so you have been told by your psychiatrist, in order to keep your brain chemistry "in proper balance," so that you do not suffer even more severe symptoms of an anxiety disorder that you seem to have inherited from your father (or so the currently dominant theory contends). None of this is cause for any particular alarm or special concern. The human condition is fraught with challenges of this nature. *Everyone* struggles with something or other. You are now a 52-year-old man, you work out on a regular basis, you have many lingering injuries from your days of combat and collision sports, and you have grown accustomed to occasional difficulties managing your anxiety. It seems as if nearly everyone you know contends with *some* type of psychological dysfunction or other. You cannot help but wonder if the pervasiveness of such disorders is not largely a function of contemporary societal conditions. Perhaps human beings are not evolutionarily suited to living in cities and large clusters of humanity. Perhaps we are all overstimulated with modern technology. Then again, maybe you just feel a bit adrift these days as you venture into the latter stages of "middle age." It seems that, as the poet says, the *center* does not quite hold. Things do seem to "fall apart" over time. You *are*, whatever else you may be, a *thing*. Life is good, though. You still prefer it to the alternative, do you not? Well, in that case, get to work and do not whimper about your back and your brain. That is about the best you can manage. Do not be dissuaded from your responsibilities by transient feelings of distress. You have it *much* better than most. *Never* forget that.

February 27, 2021

Has your culture gone completely mad, or are you simply "out of step" with the norms and mores of the society that surrounds you? These possibilities are *not*, of course, mutually exclusive. Perhaps you seek more and more distance from popular culture and the common narratives of the day *because* they are saturated with stupidity, silliness, dishonesty, and degeneracy. The project of knowing oneself is notoriously difficult, and you cannot be overly confident that your assessment of circumstances is reliable. It *is* possible that the defect lies within *you*. This possibility should not be ignored or thrust aside merely on the grounds that you seem sane enough by *your own* lights. The world is, after all, *full* of delusional people who do not *realize* that they are delusional. When you observe a nation and a culture that you simply do not recognize as "yours" in any sense beyond geography and happenstance, you ought to spend some time and effort trying to figure out what, if anything, can be done about this situation. You certainly cannot drag your society back to a condition of sanity and honesty. For practical reasons, you cannot *leave* it. It may be that your only viable option is to take the "inward turn," and detach your interests from the external world as much as is possible. It seems crazy out there. There are no signs of rationality breaking out any time soon. So, step back and let it be. Try to remain indifferent to the decline and collapse of the place you once loved. It is, as far as you can tell, beyond salvation. How about *you*? Do you think that you are *also* beyond salvation? Of course, it is not entirely clear what would constitute salvation for either you *or* your culture. Perhaps the whole notion of salvation is nothing more than a chimera. Maybe it is a fictitious condition conjured up from a desperation to avoid the inevitable decline unto death and dissolution. You cannot really claim great confidence to the contrary. At root, you just do not *know* what is coming. That assessment appears to be inescapable. You may as well get comfortable about *not* knowing. Your ignorance is broad and deep. In this, you are certainly *not* alone.

February 28, 2021

People who are enamored of certainty should probably stick to mathematics. Even the empirical sciences cannot offer certainty about the spatiotemporal world. David Hume was fairly persuasive on this score. You cannot, therefore, help but find the *demand* for certainty baffling when it comes to claims about transcendent phenomena such as God, the soul, or some form of an afterlife. Of course, all positive claims regarding such matters *could* be mere projections conjured up by terrified talking apes who are desperate to deny death and extinction. The demand for conclusive proof that God either does or does not exist is requiring more than the subject matter permits. It is a bit like insisting upon conclusive proof that the future will resemble the past, or that the next advance in technology will make the world a happier place. It does no good to reject uncertainty about areas of consideration for which certainty is simply not available. No one would ever make another child if antecedent proof of the child's long, happy life were required. There are lots and lots of things that you will never know for certain, and others that you will never know until it is too late to change the crucial conditions. This is neither a defect in the world, nor is it a deficiency on your part. This is the way that the world works. Learn what you can, but do not insist upon understanding *everything*. You must move forward despite your ignorance. You may stumble. In fact, it *almost* certain that you *will* stumble. Try not to let that bother you.

March 1, 2021

If you fail to learn from your observations of the people around you and the events that transpire right in front of you, then you *deserve* to suffer the consequences of that failure. What are you doing allowing experience to unfold without extracting anything of value from it? You may not be entirely certain whether life has some transcendent meaning or purpose, but you *must* realize that learning as much as you can is one of the primary functions you can perform in this lifetime as a human being. Consider how unlikely it is that this universe would allow you to exist as a creature endowed with the capacity to *reason* about what you see, hear, and otherwise experience. Your brain works (for the most part). What a shame it would be to sleepwalk your way through an existence that could have been far richer, far deeper, and far more thoroughly *lived*. You begin to improve your character *only* if you think carefully about what you experience and what you can *learn* from your experience. The poorly lived lives are not terribly difficult to identify. When you encounter a catastrophic life, aim to be *unlike* the person living it. Begin by moving away from failure, and continue by finding your way toward virtue and excellence. If you are not striving to become better, then you are frittering away a great gift and a singular opportunity. In this, you are not alone. The world is *filled* with frittering.

March 2, 2021

You are older at this moment than you have ever been before. This is *not* a novel state of affairs. That has been true every moment you have lived, but it has not seemed particularly urgent before the relatively recent past and the present. Perhaps "urgent" is not the optimal word, but you cannot deny that you are beginning to *feel* age in a way that you had not previously noticed. The aches and pains have been with you for *many* years. Combat and collision sports were great fun and enormously exciting in your youth, but you now realize that the damage you sustained, and the lasting consequences of thousands of crushing impacts cannot be rationally justified in retrospect. In other words, you realized long ago that you would suffer much less nagging pain today had you never gotten involved in football, wrestling, and boxing. As a teenager, you probably lacked the cognitive wherewithal and the informed perspective to appreciate the future suffering to which you were subjecting your body. Football, in particular, has done things to your back and neck that ought not to have been done. None of this, however, is quite what you are experiencing now. Even if you had not sustained the injuries in question, there would still be something nagging at you about being closer to one hundred years into your sojourn on this planet than you are to your first day out in the open air. Is this, perhaps, what the early whisper of your mortality feels like? Has death moved close enough for you to sense its presence? Maybe that *is* what you feel. Maybe death has taken a stroll a little nearer to you than you had ever noticed before. Then again, your experience may be nothing more than the consequences of accumulated wear and tear. You have absorbed more years than did many significant historical figures. You have, for example, outlived St. Thomas Aquinas. Here you remain for the time being. So, *now* what?

March 3, 2021

How many Americans are dumb enough to believe that politicians actually care about the people of the nation? No one ever ran for office because of a deep and abiding love for the people or impulse to pursue their interests. Of course many of them will *say* things like that during a campaign, but it takes a colossal dimwit to process such nonsense as anything other than pandering. It is one thing to observe and assess the credulity of the general public, but it is something else entirely to allow yourself to become upset about the masses and their attitudes. What good will it do you, or anyone else for that matter, to grind your teeth because you are surrounded by a large number of gullible twits? Has it not always been thus with humanity, and does it not promise to remain thus for as long as humans strut and fret their way through the world? Socrates was prosecuted by three craven charlatans, and he was executed due to the vote of an Athenian majority. The general populace has not improved morally or intellectually in the interim from then to now. The public of *your* nation probably will not even *bother* to kill you. Why *would* they, after all? Surely, you realize that you are no Socrates. You are not even worth the time and trouble of a prosecution (probably). Do not expect to be martyred to the cause of reason and justice. Just expect to be ignored and relegated to obscurity. That will do nicely, will it not?

March 4, 2021

Why do so many of the talking apes believe that they are capable of understanding *everything*? Within the last 24 hours, you have heard three separate and mutually incompatible predictions about the economy in 2021, and all three were delivered with roughly equivalent overconfidence. Can economists simply *never* admit that they have *no* idea what is going to happen over the short *or* long term? The case is even worse when it comes to the so-called "climate scientists," and their relentless cries that the sky is falling, the globe is warming, the climate is "changing" (to go *way* out on *that* limb), and everything detrimental to life on the planet is due, either entirely or in large part, to the irrational heedlessness of the human race. Of course, the other talking apes mostly seem *not* to heed, much to their consternation, the ceaseless bleating of the climate science "community." Perhaps spending a century or so insisting, "The end is nigh," has undermined the credibility of the "experts" in the relevant fields, or maybe it is just obvious that *no one* has *any* idea what anyone is supposed to *do* about the (alleged) problem. In another hundred years, the same "community" will bleat the same alarm — in repackaged terminology (unless, of course, everyone is dead by then). No one will pay attention. On the other hand, what do *you* know about the climate? Luckily, you will be dead for most of the future. At least you will not have to keep listening to the alarmists screeching.

March 5, 2021

The sum total of all human suffering at any moment in time is too staggering to contemplate in earnest. Consider the starvation and malnutrition currently afflicting Sub-Saharan Africa or Southeast Asia. The cries of infants and toddlers that will never reach your ears is sufficient to stop your imagination in its tracks. You cannot comprehend the conditions against which much of the world is forced to contend on a daily basis. You are, to put the matter bluntly, *spoiled* by wealth, excess, and luxury that many of your fellow Earthlings probably cannot hope to experience in their lifetimes. Should you feel guilty because of your good fortune? Would *that* do anyone else any good? Are you obligated to drop everything and devote the rest of your life to alleviating as much human suffering as you can manage? Even if you are, you know that you are *not*, in fact, going to *do* any such thing. You are going to continue living your life more or less as you have been living it. You are going to tend to the satisfaction of your own desires and the maximization of the preferences of your family members. You are going to look out for *yourself*, *your* spouse, and *your* kids. The rest of the world can look after itself (or not). Does this mean that you do not *really* care about all of the suffering that you currently contemplate? Perhaps it does. You have no justification for ruling this explanation "out of bounds" merely because you might find it disturbing. Anyone can *claim* to care about the suffering of others, and nearly everyone does, in fact, make this claim when pressed. Such claims are, of course, not *even* a dime a dozen. Indeed, they can be had for *free*, can they not? All the world shrugs, and congratulates itself for the depth of the concern thereby expressed. The shrug says all there is to say. Thus, the humans can sleep at night.

March 6, 2021

It seems that more and more people are voluntarily indulging in a form of sensory deprivation with respect to their immediate physical environment. They are walking around wearing headphones or earbuds, and they are listening to music rather than paying attention to the sounds surrounding them in the actual environment through which they pass. This is a particularly bad idea given that they cannot hear anything coming up from *behind* them. This is simply a recipe for tragic experience. They are not exactly *begging* to be victimized by street thugs, but they are certainly turning themselves into soft, easy targets for assault (or worse). Although you are tempted to mention the problem to strangers that you see engaged in this unwise behavior, you are fairly confident that none of them would want to hear your opinions concerning this matter, and you are also somewhat ambivalent about the consequences to which they seem to insist upon subjecting themselves. Maybe this is one of those lessons that certain people just insist upon learning the hard way. Who are *you*, after all, to deprive them of the relevant experience? Pain and suffering *are* the most effective teachers, are they not? With the exception of your family members, perhaps it is best to sit back, say nothing, and allow everyone to "learn at their own pace" about the dangers of failing to *pay attention*. Sooner or later, just about everyone learns this lesson — one way or another. Well, some "learn" only in the experience of getting *killed*.

March 7,2021

Whatever else it may accomplish, having life insurance tends to incentivize your murder, does it not? Probably no one is going to kill you in order to collect the insurance money, but if there *were no* insurance money, then that would be one less motive to do you in. There are, of course, plenty of other reasons that various people might want to kill you, but why multiply such temptations beyond necessity? Perhaps the best of all possible worlds involves taking out a life insurance policy on yourself, but not telling anyone about it. This way, when you drop dead, your loved ones will have their grief dampened somewhat by a surprise windfall. The relevant mechanisms can be set up in secret using lawyers and insurance agencies. So, although a husband and father may have been *lost*, a significant sum of money will have been *found*. That is not exactly a poke in the eye with a sharp stick. Though none of the parties in question will admit it, you can be fairly certain that they would prefer your death coupled with a bundle of money to your death coupled with *nothing*. These people are not *stupid*, after all. Unfortunately, everyone already knows about your life insurance, and there is no plausible explanation for allowing it to lapse. Alas, one or more of them may conspire to murder you and collect. So it goes. You knew the risks, did you not?

March 8, 2021

Something involving members of the British Royal Family evidently occurred today. The talking heads on television and the Internet are blathering about some kind of Prince or Princess or some other "Royal" for some reason. You can only rock back slightly in your seat and wonder how there are still Kings, Queens, Princes, Princesses, and the other various forms of royal figures in the world. Are people *really* still doing this? How does anyone utter the expression, "Your Highness," or "Your Majesty" with a straight face? This weird atavistic streak apparently infects several different societies. It is not *only* the British who remain susceptible to this bizarre taxonomic quirk of identifying certain groups of human beings as "special" due to their membership in a particular clan. It is as if members of the families in question are somehow endowed with magical properties merely for being born into, or for marrying into, a group of relations. They are afforded an enormous deference by large segments of the public, and nearly *everything* they do is treated as if it is inherently and uniquely fascinating. This is all simply baffling. They are possessed of no special innate talents or intellectual prowess. They are just "royal" for largely historical reasons. The Emperor may have no clothes, but he still seems to have plenty of relatives. You can only hope that, behind closed doors, these Princes and Princesses are having a good laugh and wondering how these lives they live are still possible.

March 9, 2021

The United States economy appears to teeter on the brink of some type of socio-economic collapse. You have no idea when it will come, how bad it will be, how long it will last, or what the long-term consequences might be. Indeed, you do not even know for certain that it *is* coming at all, but the current indications point in the direction of trouble ahead. Try to remain indifferent to all of those conditions over which you have no control. There is nothing you can do about monetary policy, the Federal Reserve, or the performance of the stock or bond markets. Let all of that business unfold as it will, and do not allow yourself to become apprehensive about any of it. Prepare for what you think you see coming. Stock up on shelf-stable food supplies, because it looks like the price of groceries is getting ready to skyrocket. Inflation does not impact the food that is already *in your house*. Make sure that you have abundant supplies of everything that is necessary for survival. Water purifiers may come in handy if the stuff that comes out of the tap ceases to be potable. Canned food is edible *indefinitely* as long as it is properly stored. You would prefer that guns and ammo will *not* be needed, but you had better have those on hand in case your preferences do not conform to future events. Look into the cost of a generator in case of prolonged power outages. Store up medical supplies, and brush up on your ability to treat burns, breaks, and lacerations. You have no way of knowing what services will continue to be available, and you do not know what anything is going to cost during the economic disruption that seems to hover on the horizon. Get *your* affairs in order. Make sure that *your* family can make it through the coming trials. If you can do that while also helping others, then do so. If your resources dwindle, then the family comes *first*. Do everything in your power to meet the needs that you *can* meet, and do not fret about anything that lies beyond your control. Rational indifference to the world "out there" must guide your decisions. You are not in charge of the world. Mind your own house. Protect your own family as best you can. The rest is *not* up to you. The world will probably keep turning.

March 10, 2021

The Federal Reserve and the federal government are conjuring "money" out of thin air yet again, and you cannot help but expect inflation to follow almost as if a law of nature governs the relevant processes. Perhaps you are poorly informed about economics, and you certainly have no formal training in the area, but *trillions* of new dollars entering the available pool of money, and doing so without anyone having produced goods or provided services in order to *earn* any of that money seems to guarantee that the dollars in your pocket, and in your bank account, will now have far less purchasing power. There is no particular reason, as far as you can tell, to expect the deleterious consequences of *inventing* trillions of dollars to abate any time soon. In other words, it seems that the politicians and their lackeys have ensured that the value of your money, not to mention the value of every other American's money, will decline and remain diminished for years to come. The economy is not likely to recover any time soon, and the nation may well find itself facing something like another *Great Depression*. Either that, or nothing particularly terrible is going to happen, and all of the doomsayers (including yourself) are going to be shocked by happy days ahead. As usual, you really do not know where this nation and its culture are going or what the future holds. There it is. Here it comes.

March 11, 2021

Evidently, you are supposed to be concerned about the "immorality" of inequality as well as about its destabilizing effect on society. This is, of course, laughably *stupid*. Nature does *not* make; indeed it *cannot* make, *equal* creatures. No two organisms are endowed with equivalent capacities, needs, or utility to the world at large. Each creature is simply *different* from every other creature. This difference is, and always has been, *incommensurable*. It makes no sense to ask whether, for example, dogs and cats are "equal." What is the interest at stake? If you want a pet that will deter burglars, then dogs are superior to cats (for the most part — chihuahuas notwithstanding). If, on the other hand, you want a pet that you do not need to walk on a daily basis, then you are better off with a cat. The same "inequalities" apply to your own species as well. Are you deeply concerned that your son may never have the opportunity to *give birth*? Does he *want* that particular "opportunity," and is he "oppressed" by its absence? It seems that brain surgeons are more richly compensated for their professional efforts than are cashiers at the local grocery store. Is this an "injustice," or is it a simple acknowledgment that the former occupation is far more difficult and far less readily replaceable than is the latter? Wealthy people can, if they choose, purchase luxury vehicles whereas poor people cannot. So it goes. Is everyone "entitled" to own a Rolls Royce? If so, *why*? No two intellects are "equal" in any significant sense, and differences in intellectual prowess are liable to result in differences in, among other things, living standards and earning power. There is precisely *no* reason that this should *not* be so. Professional athletes make *much* more money, in general, than do those who are less gifted in the relevant areas. This is *not* unjust. They are *better* at doing something that society, for whatever reason, remunerates more richly than sweeping and mopping. Humming birds seldom kill eagles. This is not a moral *flaw* in nature. This is not *wrong*. Humans are, whatever *else* they may be, *animals*. There are "wolves" among us, and there are "sheep" as well. Nothing can or should be done to "correct" this condition. The sheep resent the wolves, and the wolves find the sheep delicious. *Vive La différence*!

March 12, 2021

It *ought* to make *no* difference to you whether other people behave in noble and admirable fashion or not. Who are *you*, after all, that you should concern yourself about the manner in which others comport themselves? No one vested you with the authority to govern other persons, you were not elected to any Office of Public Integrity, and you have not been selected to function as one of God's modern prophets. You can admit that you *struggle* with this particular element of minding your own business, and you frequently feel the desire to smack some sense into imbeciles whom you encounter in person and those whom you see and hear on television and the Internet. Until you are able to extirpate this type of impulse, however, you would probably be better off *not* encountering quite so many

imbeciles. Since you lack the
capacity to reduce their
numbers by fiat, the wiser
and more efficient course of
action would seem to be
spending far less time in
pursuits that entail the
temptation to backhand
idiots. There may be a
greater challenge here than
meets the eye, given that the
world's supply of morons
seems to be increasing at a
rate that outpaces the rate
at which global population
expands. This may be
attributable to one of
nature's little jokes or to
(a lack of) nurture, but
questions of etiology are
immaterial to your pursuit of
abiding peace of mind.
Whatever the causes, "they"
are certainly "out there,"
and the simplest course of
action, for the time being,
is to spend as little time
"out there" yourself as is
compatible with your survival
and your psychological
health. The recent months of

lockdown and isolation have been, all things considered, something of a blessing in disguise in your case. You have had no viable alternative to avoiding the dimwits and the depraved. Were you not mostly imprisoned in your home, is there not a fair chance that you would have been imprisoned as a "guest of the state" by this time? That would *not*, you can only guess, facilitate your tranquility. Stay home a bit longer. Spend less time watching television and surfing the Internet. Read books, take care of your yard, do a lot of pushups, and enjoy the solitude that attends the pandemic. You can (and should) shrug at the *entire* external world in *one* fell swoop.

March 13, 2021

You are looking forward to watching the cage fights tonight. Some interesting matchups should be on offer, and some highly skilled combat athletes are going to try to dismantle each other, and render each other unconscious for your entertainment. Some of your friends and family members regard this as a "barbaric" sport. Well, it had damn well better be! That is, after all, the real point of the exercise, is it not? Of course you appreciate the skills involved, and you marvel at the discipline required of the fighters who engage at *this* level of expertise. None of this is lost on you. The rigors of training in multiple martial arts, and the adversity to which these athletes are willing to subject themselves is simply astonishing. You respect and admire them.

Nonetheless, you want to see their blood on the canvas as well. Any fan of cage fighting and other combat sports who denies this bloodlust is either very dishonest or very self-deceived. When a bone snaps, a joint dislocates, or an eye socket is lacerated open, your first impulse is to look away, but you also understand why they repeatedly broadcast the slow-motion replay of those injuries and of the hideous aftermath of each such horror. Like you, the other fans want to get as close to the blood and viscera as they can. Not many forms of entertainment can offer anything quite as primal. The *crack* of shin to skull is a call to something deep inside you. It is terrifying, and you cannot get enough of it. Do *not* deny this fascination.

4, 2021

o you *still* manage to
irritated by politicians
their media lackeys lying
to a credulous public yet
again? When imbeciles believe
liars telling *obvious* lies,
it makes no sense to get
upset about the matter.
People who pet porcupines are
apt to get quills where they
probably do not want quills.
Do not blame the porcupine
for doing what porcupines do.
Politicians lie. *All* of them
lie. It is almost certainly
impossible to win election to
any significant office
without telling the public
the lies that they want
desperately to hear. The
public absolutely *insists*
upon being lied to, and then
they make a show of decrying
the liars whom they elect on
the basis of the lies the
liars have told them. It is a
bizarre form of interaction.
A solid majority of the
voting public *refuses* to vote

for honest candidates, so the
public gets nothing but
dishonest elected officials,
and everyone complains about
the mendacity of politicians.
It is a bit like employing
the services of prostitutes,
insisting upon using only the
ones who have syphilis, and
then griping about the fact
that you have to get treated
for syphilis. No one *has* to
go to whores. The parallel
with politicians is, perhaps,
all too easily drawn. You do
not *have* to vote, and you do
not *have* to vote for a liar.
You make a fool of yourself
when you vote for a liar and
then whine about corruption
and dishonesty in politics.
Stop voting. The entire game
is corrupt, and only whores
run for office. Turn away
from that pathetic spectacle.
Let none of it trouble you
any further. Have a smoke.

March 15, 2021

If you look around and listen to various sources of information regarding your nation and its culture, then you are going to see and hear a *lot* of absolute *insanity*. One interesting question about this madness concerns whether anyone actually *believes* any of it, or whether the people spouting the insanity *know* as well as *you* know that they are making childishly stupid and indefensible claims. You struggle to imagine any adult honestly embracing a worldview so clearly at odds with incontrovertible, empirically verifiable facts. Surely, no one *believes* that men can get pregnant and give birth to human babies, right? Surely, *all* adults understand that a man does not have a womb. There is, of course, much more to rule male pregnancy "out of court," but is it really necessary to marshal a great deal of further evidence about the matter? Are there men taking birth control pills because they are "not ready" to give have babies yet? Are obstetricians preparing to deliver little "bundles of joy" from the male birth canal? If so, then is someone developing the necessary medical equipment (whatever that might entail)? It simply *cannot* be so. You want to say that it *must* not be so, but that introduces a needless semantic and conceptual muddle where you seek clarity. No, it simply *cannot* be so. If you are wrong about this, then it is time to begin drinking much more heavily. Of course, if there *are* people who actually *believe* this sort of nonsense, then you really should not trouble yourself about them. They are unworthy even of a raised eyebrow. Avert your gaze. Do not even bother to shrug.

March 16, 2021

When did you become so prone to injury during *sleep*? Surely, this cannot be a sign of health and wellbeing in your declining years. Once you start hurting yourself while you are unconscious and barely moving, there is only so much time that can elapse before you start to suffer damage as a result of breathing both in and out. So it goes. Perhaps you need to spend more time stretching, and you should also alter your daily workout to fit in more smoothly with a body that just is not what it used to be. Are you, however, willing to accept a certain degree of physiological decline without first doing everything in your power to maintain functional health and conditioning as long as your decaying carcass allows? This has the feeling of a battle against age and time, and only a fool believes he stands a chance against those two formidable foes. No one has ever "won" that fight. There is, however, something noble about engaging in the struggle as best you are able, and there is something creditable about trying to be a "tough old guy" for another handful of years (or more if you can manage it). Try not to allow vanity to cause stupid decisions in your pursuit of the relevant goals. Trying to exercise like you did when you were 25 is not going to end well. Your joints, muscles, ligaments, and tendons simply cannot bear the same strain these days. Getting old is not for quitters. Of course, getting *dead* is, ultimately, for everyone. So, try not to take the aging "thing" personally. Remember, it only lasts until you die.

March 17, 2021

One of the interesting things you have noticed about the current lockdown and pandemic is the degree to which you have *not* missed the company of other people. Of course, you never were much of a "people person," and you find most members of your species to be either vaguely annoying or uninteresting altogether, but it is at least a little surprising that your periodic interactions with just one or two other persons is more than enough to satisfy your interests in this area. Perhaps you are not quite the "social creature" that philosophers and social "scientists" have so frequently claimed. It might just be the boring people with no interesting thoughts of their own who are in such desperate need of regular socializing. Indeed, have you not noticed that the people who are (allegedly) the "most fun" to be around are also the most vapid and hollow members of your species? These are the kinds of people who actually *enjoy* attending baseball games (somehow). Have you ever met anyone who "loves a crowd," but was also a worthwhile interlocutor over lunch, dinner, or drinks shared between only *two* persons? There is all the difference in the world between a *person* and *people*. Get more than three persons together in a room, and you will have *people* (unfortunately). Even if you like and respect each person in that collective, the collective *itself* is something you would prefer to avoid if at all possible. In short, the company of others *en masse* is wildly overrated and seldom worth the requisite time and effort.

March 18, 2021

It seems that you have begun to have a recurring type of nightmare in which you realize that you are asleep, you sense the powerful impulse to escape the dream environment, but you are *unable* to wake yourself. This should not be particularly terrifying in and of itself, but there is always some accompanying *need* to wake up before a crucial deadline of one sort or another. The lives and wellbeing of loved ones always seem to hang in the balance. In one permutation of the nightmare, a family member has been abducted and will be executed (or worse) if you do not wake up and come to the rescue. In another version, you have a scheduled meeting, and failure to arrive on time will result in financial cataclysm for your family. It is never *your* life or safety that hangs in the balances in

these dream scenarios. That
would not suffice to trouble
you very much. It is always
concern about the family that
drives your deepest and most
unsettling fears. How does
anyone involved in a criminal
lifestyle, you cannot help
but wonder maintain a *family*?
How are they not constantly
horrified that one of their
rivals will do something
terrible to a spouse, a
child, a parent, or a
sibling? Surely, law
enforcement must also have
the capacity to exploit
familial bonds when they
negotiate with suspects from
whom they wish to extract
information. At least *your*
terrors are (for the time
being), eliminated once you
awaken from your slumbers.
Those whose lives and
"careers" place their
families at risk must never
enjoy of moment of genuine
peace or a full night of
satisfying and restorative
sleep. Either that or only

sociopaths can function effectively in those fields of endeavor. Can anyone sincerely shrug off *real* danger to their children? Those are psychological waters you would prefer *not* to fathom. Criminals, it would seem, *cannot* make ideal parents. Then again, perhaps *no one* can be *ideal* at all.

March 19, 2021

It seems that a new market forecaster unleashes a new prophecy of economic doom with each passing day. Inevitably, this is followed by some other market forecaster declaring that the doomsayers are misguided. You have no way of knowing whether *any* of them are correct or not. Economics is pretty far removed from your wheelhouse, after all. The interesting question concerns whether these various ominous scenarios coming to pass would actually matter to you and the manner in which you conduct your life. Given that you rarely leave your home, and seldom drive your vehicle further than a few miles, you do not have much to fear from sharply rising gasoline prices. The cost of food might skyrocket, but you have at least a two-year supply of canned goods, freeze dried meat, vegetables, pasta, rice, and fruit stored away in places about which no one else knows. You can easily double your current food storage with one bulk order from any one of several different companies that specialize in long shelf-life food and storage receptacles. You also have several water purification systems if the stuff coming out of your kitchen faucet is rendered unreliable. Finally, if things get *really* hairy, you have several firearms and about a thousand rounds of ammunition, should you find that you are compelled to defend yourself and your stockpile of food. Other contingencies for which you are *not* fully prepared can, of course, arise. You cannot anticipate *everything*. The most likely "calamities," however, should not cause you any great distress. Try to maintain an emotional distance if the economy implodes. Do not get caught up in the hysteria that will be sure to follow the implosion. Keep your head when others lose theirs. *Never* panic. It never helps to do so. Reason is the most reliable tool for dealing with the challenges that will inevitably arise.

March 20, 2021

Might it not be that the *Hebrew Bible*, the *New Testament*, and the *Quran* all tell a continuous story that is, with the removal of a few glitches and possible corruptions of texts and translations, all about the same God? Of course, it *may* well be that all of the aforementioned texts are nothing more than fictions invented by men who never had any contact with anything supernatural at all. Maybe there is no God. That *is* possible. If God *does* exist, however, and if all of the Abrahamic traditions *have* had some type of access to the truth about God and His creation, then it is possible that Jews, Christians, and Muslims all worship the same Creator. Obviously, Jesus cannot be quite what mainline Christianity claims if Judaism and Islam are correct. The two latter traditions reject the divinity of Jesus as a literal incarnation of God made flesh. Of course, it is not entirely clear that Jesus, himself, ever *claimed* to be a literal incarnation of God made flesh. Is there some way to convince all of the People of the Book, the People of the Scripture, that they are, underneath their apparent differences, practicing the *same* religion? You may not identify as a Jew, Christian, or Muslim, but you do *believe* in "their" God. The God of Abraham, Isaac, and Jacob persists throughout all of the relevant narratives. Why so much fighting and hatred among these sects? Try to make no unnecessary distinctions among the Monotheists. Let the sectarianism pass you by without getting caught up in it. There is no benefit in separating the believers into different camps.

March 21, 2021

All of the newest technological gadgetry makes it much easier for you to spend money. This *could* be a mere coincidence or an unintended consequence of various scientific developments, however, you cannot help but suspect that someone, somewhere is *trying* to make money. That is all well and good, of course. Making money by supplying goods and services that other people desire more than they desire to keep the money that they must pay in order to receive the goods and services in question is at least as American as is any apple pie. What, however, is the rational or economic justification for all of the tutorials on how to do things that no one will ever *need* to do and that you cannot figure out a reason that anyone would *want* to do? Clearly, there *are*, in fact, people who *do* want to do the things that you cannot imagine anyone wanting to do, but as justifications go, *that* is fairly thin gruel. There is, evidently, an entire economy composed of people with whom you would prefer not to associate doing things that you would prefer not to do, and various entities are raking in some significant profit from the people doing the things that you find entirely inexplicable. This is something like the economic equivalent of *dark matter*. You can tell that it is "out there," but you have no idea what it is or what, if anything, you are supposed to do about it. There is something like *gravity* at work in all this. There is no escaping it, and it surrounds you everywhere you go. It also seems vaguely "sticky." Try to avoid getting it *on* you.

March 22, 2021

You really ought to resist the temptation to get caught up in the political theatrics and the performative, phony cries of outrage that seem to have become staples of social media, and that are too frequently amplified by the "news" media. It is not *easy* to watch the pervasive degradation of a nation and a culture that you once regarded as "yours" in some meaningful sense. Observing as the stupidity metastasizes is enough to make you wish you had been born in a different place, or at a different point in history, but these are, of course, futile flights of fancy. It seems that you are going to have the *opportunity* to chronicle the death of Western Civilization and the implosion of the United States of America (unless, of course, *you* expire first), but it is entirely up to you whether you take on this task or simply turn away and leave the sad story for someone else to tell. There must have been people in roughly the same position toward the latter days of the declining Roman Empire. The collapse of an empire is not easily circumscribed in space and time. It is not as if Rome was sacked once and for all, and everyone agreed the very next day that an epoch had ended. Similarly, the death of the West will be an ill-defined affair. It is likely to resemble climate change more so than a train wreck. The decline will probably be sufficiently gradual for many to pretend that they do not see it. Well, all things pass away, do they not? Weeping will do no good. Perhaps you will get to see a bit of what comes next. Of course, not *everything* is worth the trouble of watching.

March 23, 2021

There are a lot of people who are simply unemployable in *any* job whatsoever. For some reason, there are people who regard it as inappropriate to point this out, and even more inappropriate to identify specific individuals whom you regard as likely candidates for uselessness in the marketplace. It is simply *dishonest* to pretend that you cannot tell when you are in the presence of a human being whose life is not working out and is not likely to start working out anytime soon. Look around at the rest of the animal kingdom, observe all the flora and fauna you like, and you will see all sorts of malformed organisms that have *no* chance of living long enough to procreate. Why is there a prohibition against noticing that there are lots of people who have no chance of flourishing and no chance of making any significant contribution to the sum total of human knowledge and achievement? Just start by considering *yourself* and your own paltry achievements. If you had died as a child, what would the world have lost? It is not as if you are on the cusp of curing cancer or making the next great leap in our collective understanding of quantum mechanics. You can read, write, and you have been gainfully employed for decades, but your life, in the grand scheme of things, amounts to almost nothing at all. How many human lives have amounted to, and will amount to, even *less* than yours? The number has got to be staggering. Most human lives do not matter, and yet most humans are enormously fortunate to *live* those lives. So, try not to get overly upset when things do not quite go your way. You are *not* alone. There are

plenty of people who are a
lot like you.

March 24, 2021

Evidently, you just never tire of trying to convince imbeciles and liars to acknowledge the incontrovertible facts staring them in their blank, lifeless faces. This makes *you* stupid, does it not? Who, after all, has the greater problem; the person who never admits that he is wrong, or the person who keeps getting *angry* about the *other* guy who never admits that he is wrong? Stop expecting or insisting that the worst human beings on the face of the planet must, at long last, develop integrity after they pass through a kind of extended moral puberty. You really need to give the Devil his due when it comes to these people. The idiots are his for the taking, he takes them, and he manipulates them like the mindless marionettes that they are. They do his bidding because they never had any idea what else they could have done. When it comes to the intellectually sophisticated liars, however, you ought to recognize not only that the Devil has his hooks deeply sunk into these professional prevaricators, but also that *they* are gleeful, *voluntary* participants in this relationship. They *know* what they are doing. They *like* lying. They willingly and happily *embrace* evil. He owns them because they *want* him to own them. It is not as if they are being dragged kicking and screaming to Hell. They asked directions! Indeed, they are so impatient to do the Devil's work that they are not even willing to wait to go to Hell *after* they drop dead. No, they are doing everything in their power to instantiate Hell right *here* on Earth. In fact, they are not even content to live in their own subdivision of Hell on Earth. They absolutely insist that *you* must *join* them, and *you* must submit to their dark Overlord just as they have. These are the people who do everything in their power to facilitate pedophiles, pederasts, abortionists, sex traffickers, and rapists of every conceivable variety, and they are willing to tell *any* lie in service of these nefarious ends. Why do you allow these minions of Satan to trouble *you*? That is precisely what they *want*. Your misery is like *music* to these people. You can fight against them without allowing them into your psyche during the battle. *You* do the right thing. Do not trouble yourself about Satan's Little Helpers.

March 25, 2021

The thing that stands out about all of the alleged sightings of unidentified flying craft with maneuverability that far outstrips anything any current military seems to have, is not the technological wizardry described. The thing that stands out is the description of the beings who allegedly pilot these craft. They are almost always described as morphologically humanoid. In other words, they look like a lot like *people*. Generally, they are described as smaller than the average human being, and they seem to have larger eyes than we do, but they are symmetrical beings with two arms, two legs, two eyes, a nose and mouth along the centerline of the face, etc. Does this not indicate, as clearly as anything could, that they are from *this* planet? Unless evolutionary theory is completely divorced from reality, there is virtually no chance that living beings from another planet would evolve the same basic body type that we find among members of our own species. A different planet, with a different mass, gravitational environment, distribution of elements, and a (presumably) very different series of antecedent events leading to the development of life, would *never* produce environmental pressures to render basic humanoid features the most adaptable to the vastly different environment on this other world. Perhaps the entire UFO phenomenon is hokum and hoax. If not, however, the humanoid structure of the "aliens" indicates that they are Earthlings. If they are from the future, then it seems that our descendants will survive for some time. This is good news, right? So, there is no good reason to worry about "them" destroying "us." They *are* us! Either that, or all of these alleged sightings are a bunch of silly nonsense fabricated by charlatans, or by people with overactive imaginations. If the whole narrative is simply made up, then we again have nothing to fear from the "aliens" because they are *fictitious*. So, the *great* probability is that the UFO "pilots" are either imaginary, or they are human descendants from this planet's future. In either case, we probably have nothing to fear. Finally, if "they" wanted to "do us in," would they not have managed it by now? If you ever see a UFO, just wave and do not fret about the matter.

March 26, 2021

It is essential that you know your weaknesses, that you acknowledge them, and that you do everything in your power to improve your character as best you can. Indeed, this is your *primary* purpose. What else can you accomplish if you fail to do the work necessary to attain wisdom and virtue? If you lack wisdom, then you cannot reliably tell good from evil, skillful from unskillful conduct, or righteousness from transgression. If you lack virtue, then you will be unable to perform good deeds, and you will be unable to resist the temptation to perpetrate evil. Such temptations assail humanity in *relentless* fashion. Scripture tells you that sin crouches always at your door. Whether you believe in God or not, and whether you take the term "sin" literally or merely as a metaphor indicating evil, unskillful, or deleterious conduct, surely you must prefer to be a good person to being a lousy human being. You *cannot* reject that distinction *entirely*. You have *preferences*, do you not? What you prefer, you must regard (at least at the moment of preference) as *better*, in *some* sense, than states to which you are averse. Doing what you believe to be better is up to *you*, is it not? Focus your energy on doing better rather than worse. As for all of the conditions that you cannot control, what benefit do you find in obsessing about such matters? Do not perseverate. Observe, learn, and move forward. This is the best you can do where the external world is concerned. No more than this can be required of you, nor should you ask more than this of anyone else. Indeed, you ought to ask as little of others as possible.

March 27, 2021

The more you learn about Islam, the more you realize how badly you misunderstood this religion and its practitioners for *so* many years. Muslims have a fascinating scripture, and the moral code they embrace is at *least* as impressive as is any other you have encountered in any tradition presented through religion or philosophy. You have seen and heard so much misleading propaganda about Islam that you have to wonder if there is not some type of organized effort to confuse the public at large about what most Muslims *actually* believe. There is as much beauty and wisdom in the *Quran* as there is in the *Torah* or the *Gospels*. Let this realization be a lesson to you. Never judge *any* tradition or any culture by reference to the characterizations offered by persons who are not part of the religion, the culture, or the tradition in question. If you want to learn what Islam has to offer, then you *must* read its scripture *yourself*, and you must speak to (and *listen* to) people who have devoted their lives to Islam, to Allah, and to the moral code thereby enjoined upon them. What a shame it is that you have come to this understanding so late in your life. You have been so *very* wrong for so very long. Whether Muslims have the "right story" or not, they certainly have a more interesting and more constructive worldview than you ever realized. Theirs is a far deeper well from which to draw than you might have imagined. If only all the People of the Scripture could work together. Imagine what they could accomplish *together*. Ah, the "mysterious ways," and all that.

March 28, 2021

If God exists, then He must surely laugh at the stupidities of humankind, or He must surely have our extermination long since planned. Of course, you do not *know* for certain that God exists, and if there *is* a God, then you must confess that you cannot possibly know what God intends or what does and does not tickle the Creator's funny bone (if that expression is permissible). Perhaps the Apocalypse will descend upon the world tomorrow, and it might well be that thousands and thousands of years remain for the talking apes to cavort and explore the wonders of the universe. You do *not* know what is coming. It is very unwise to fall prey to the species of arrogance that convinces far too many people that they can predict the future with comfort and confidence. Unless you are granted a revelation from God, you should not be overly confident about where events are heading. Indeed, it is probably best for you not to be overly certain about anything involving the relationship between the talking apes and the transcendent realm. Stick to working on your own character. The rest is either up to God, or subject to governance by the laws of nature, or perhaps it is all just the result of chance, caprice, and randomness. In any event, all of the conditions "out there" are certainly *not* up to *you*. Stop pretending that you know what is going on or why. Stop posing as a prophet of the contemporary world. You are just another talking ape. Nothing is quite so ludicrous as is an arrogant primate.

March 29, 2021

There is a great deal of confusion about the fundamental nature of good and evil. Indeed, you seem to meet ever more people who do not accept the distinction between good and evil as a legitimate separation of two *real* and separate categories. In other words, you keep encountering people who claim that they do *not* believe in *moral* facts. Perhaps some of these people are simply behaving as contrarians, or maybe they speak mostly for the sake of shocking the sensibilities of those whom they regard as "normal" folk. A significant number of these nihilists, however, seem to be quite sincere in their rejection of the very *concepts* of moral good and evil. They seem actually to believe in *nothing* where decency and indecency are concerned. If this inclination is on the

ascendency in the nation and
culture within which you
reside, then can you continue
to *defend* that nation or that
culture with a clear
conscience? For most of your
life, you have believed that
you have a moral obligation
to defend "your" nation if it
comes under threat, but you
now perceive that the
greatest threats are, and
probably always have been,
internal to the nation and
its culture. Many of the
legal citizens of the nation
appear to be morally
repugnant and entirely
unworthy of any defense. They
seek to destroy what you once
loved because they understand
nothing of honor or decency.
The decadence and depravity
surround you everywhere you
turn. It looks and sounds
like death throes. It also
looks and sounds like
punishment. The wrath of God,
perhaps leaves humankind to
its own devices. Desolation

invariably follows. So it goes.

March 30, 2021

It seems that there is a new stupidity "going viral" throughout the culture with each passing day. If we are not being asked to pretend that men can be women (and vice-versa), then we are told that "systematic oppression" is the reason for every failure and every lousy life that accomplishes nothing, or someone declares that there are no objective facts, and we each "construct our own reality," or some other equally idiotic asseveration. The regnant priests of the new religion of moral inversion *dare* anyone to stand up and point to the patent lunacy of their every assertion, and it seems that *very* few of your fellow citizens are willing to declare that these priests are wearing no clothes. The charlatans, liars, and lunkheads stand naked before us, and they declare that it is the rest of us who are unclothed. Somehow, though, it seems that *they* are winning. The Idiot Brigade is on the march, and the rest of us appear to be content to make way, kneel before them, and allow them to breach the citadel at the center of "our" culture. Look, they have you resorting to needless metaphors in describing the circumstances you find all around you. Plain speaking and simple truth telling are now insufficient to explain the tortured state of cultural *unreality* as it currently stands. Not only does the center not hold, but it seems that there is *no center* at all. There is only bafflement and chaos. Perhaps it has always been so, and you have never noticed it before. Now, you *cannot* miss it. Maybe this is reason for gratitude after all.

March 31, 2021

Anyone who suggests that you have a moral obligation to tolerate persons or behaviors that you find to be entirely intolerable is, at the very least, *not* to be trusted. Arguably, you ought to regard any such person as an *enemy*. It may even be necessary for you actively to oppose such persons, the organizations to which they belong, and you must be prepared to resort to any means necessary to forestall the advance of *indefensible* tolerance. Look at the damage that has been done to contemporary society by the tacit decision to put up with behavior that ought to have been met with contempt and derision, at the very least, and some of which should have been met with the full power and authority of agents of the state to arrest, try, and convict the persons engaged in the behaviors in question. Those who riot, loot, and perpetrate assault against complete strangers should be arrested in *every* case, and they should spend *many* years in prison in *every* case. All too often, the race, ethnicity, sex, or ideological affiliation of the perpetrators and of the victims becomes part of the process of assessing the plainly criminal conduct that you witness. Far too many violent criminals avoid prison simply because they are protected by the current powers running the legal system. In other cases, innocent people have been convicted solely on the basis of race or affiliation with the "wrong" socio-political entities. Justice will never be served in such cases. You know that you are *not entitled* to a just world. Where you see injustice about which you can do nothing, a shrug may be the best you can manage. Is *that* the nature of tragedy?

April 1, 2021

April Fool's Day is beginning to seem a little bit redundant, is it not? Amid the "woke" and the otherwise hypersensitive and irrational cry-bully scolds, there are precious *few* days that are not devoted to foolishness. Indeed, you have wondered if there is not some type of perverse competition to come up with the most moronic form of phony outrage, or if there is not some attempt to convince more people than any other charlatan to pledge allegiance to an utterly outrageous system of inverted "values" and devote themselves to subjects of inexplicably maniacal interest. It seems that the new book burners are now dictating to the heretofore rational adults which topics of discourse are permissible and which forms of communication are to be punished. When did so much of the public at large agree to take their moral cues from the most loathsome and most dishonest human beings ever to have befouled God's creation? The expression "God's creation" is, of course, on the list of impermissible expressions. It must surely be racist, or sexist, of homophobic, or otherwise indicative of a deep character flaw afflicting the speaker. If you were to hold up a potato and say, "This is a potato," then you would, without question, face accusations of transphobia, or elitism, or sympathy for the Nazi party. The accusations need not have even the slightest plausibility or connection with reality, of course. The purpose is *intimidation*. You must say *only* what the Woke Mob permits you to say, or your career and life *must* be ruined. Honestly, such ruination, if you are to be honest, would not be entirely unwelcome. Indeed, there must something liberating about being cast out from the "polite society" of lunatics and pathological liars. Once you are officially excommunicated, you will be free to do as you please. No one will pay any attention to you ever again. Is that *not* an improvement? Embrace the mantle of the nobody. It is *so* much more satisfying than is the futile effort of trying to convince idiots and liars to improve themselves. Leave them be. Time and space will ultimately swallow everyone anyway.

April 2, 2021

You cannot help but notice the increasing frequency with which you find mystery wounds and unexplained aches throughout your body. Several times each month, you notice a bruise or abrasion on your face and you have no memory of its cause or of the moment the injury occurred. It is *just there,* out of *nowhere.* Nearly every other day your back and neck cry out for attention, and you typically cannot pinpoint the activity that caused the damage or the time period during which the injury was done. The many years of your youth and adolescence devoted to combat and collision sports are almost certainly part of the explanation. The human body, it seems, is less than perfectly designed to endure boxing, wrestling, and football. When you were young, lots of people warned you that you would pay the price as you got older. You did not exactly *disbelieve* these claims, but you did not *heed* the relevant warnings either. It is one thing to understand the probable consequences of your actions, but it is something else altogether to embrace that understanding and act accordingly. You did *not* act accordingly. You acted like you were indestructible. Many young men make this mistake, and many of them regret that mistake as older men. So, it seems that you are very much like a lot of other nitwits who wrecked their bodies doing things that were obviously contrary to their long-term interests. If you had it to do over again, would you have avoided the unnecessary damage? Certainly not *all* of it. Perhaps the wounds and pains are a bit less mysterious after all. You are, alas, just something of an idiot. You are not alone in *this* either.

April 3, 2021

You have been observing the humans for several decades now, and you ought to admit that you have almost no sense of what they are trying to accomplish. Of course, you have seen them go to work, go to school, get married, have children, grow old, and drop dead, but it is not clear that any of these activities are designed or intended to be part of the overarching endeavor of *living a life*. All of the aforementioned projects and behaviors are, to be sure, part and parcel of leading human lives, but the purpose of the living *itself*, and the associated goals here on this planet for a relatively brief period of time are still unclear from your vantage point. The fact that you are *one of* the humans does not make the rest of them any less baffling. It seems that nearly everyone works at some occupation or other, and at several *different* occupations in many cases, from young adulthood until fairly old age, and it appears that the primary benefits derived from all of that work are merely material. Houses, automobiles, food, and recreation are purchased with the proceeds of the labors associated with the jobs. Sometimes, people make some passing reference to "satisfaction" derived from working, and *some* of them *might* be telling the truth, but the vast majority of the jobs that must be done, seem to you to be entirely unsatisfying expenditures of time and energy. Some people work, for example, in *toll booths*. *That* endows life with an additional gradation of meaning? Perhaps such things are *possible*. Someone, however, must be somewhat *less* than brutally honest about what is really going on here. Befuddling business this is.

April 4, 2021

Easter is upon you, and you are struck, once again, by the oddity of the Easter Bunny and the eggs of many colors. Unlike Santa Claus, the Easter Bunny seems a thinly-drawn character and a bit of an enigma. Everyone knows where Santa lives, how he gets into the houses, and the transport that gets him around the planet. The Easter Bunny, on the other hand, seems to have no fixed address, is not generally presumed to use the chimney as access to homes, and possesses no canonical conveyance whereby he makes his appointed rounds. Indeed, do you even *know* for certain that the Easter Bunny is *male*? Santa Claus has a beard and a wife. For all you can tell, the Easter Bunny is single, and you have never encountered any observable physiological evidence to indicate sex or gender. How *does* this enormous, androgenous, intelligent, (possibly homeless) creature carry eggs, chocolate, and marshmallow chicks, in a woven basket, while children are *not* supposed to be terrified of this phenomenon? What explains the *size* of this rabbit? Was it, perhaps, exposed to radiation? If so, then why is it not green? So much remains incomplete about the Easter Bunny legend, but we are expected to remain blissfully ignorant and entirely passive about the matter. The bunny delivers chocolates shaped like bunnies, and we are supposed to look the other way at this apparent vicarious cannibalism. The whole thing is simply outrageous. Can this culture not produce better myths than this? The story of the Easter Bunny simply *reeks* of sloth. Do not even get started on the absence of any connection to

the concept of resurrection.
Such a shame. *So* lazy.

April 5, 2021

Secularism *is* a type of faith, is it not? Though some may regard it as the *absence* of faith, secularism is only a viable worldview on the presupposition that there is *no* God, or that there is, at the very least, no God who *cares* about what we do as individuals or as collectives. You cannot, of course, *know* with absolute certainty that God does *not* exist. *No one* can know such a thing with absolute certainty. Atheists and secularists are, therefore, acting on a belief, or a *hope*, that there will be no punishment for their failure to conduct themselves in accordance with God's commands. It is *possible* that they are correct, and it is *possible* that they are incorrect. Analogously, the "person of faith" believes or hopes that there is a God, or some other transcendent foundation of the world that we experience, and of the moral facts by which most of us believe we are bound. Perhaps those of us who believe in God are correct, and perhaps we are incorrect. You have never been granted a revelation or experienced God in any direct or verifiable fashion. It may be that *no one* has *ever* had a verifiable experience of the divine. We are, *all* of us, placing wagers with the lives that we lead. There is no way to avoid placing these wagers. So, place your bet, try your best, and never fall prey to the suggestion that your approach to living in this world is inherently less rationally defensible than is the approach of the faithless. Everyone acts in accordance with some form of faith or other. You choose yours and you move forward as necessary. Choosing *no* faith is *not* an option.

April 6, 2021

Consider how much of the phenomenon that gets passed off as "history" must be afflicted by the same dishonesty and incompetence that plagues the "news" as reported by the current "mainstream" media. You cannot remember the last time you encountered a "news" report that was true, interesting, and ideologically unbiased. The corporations and government entities that control the media clearly have a preferred narrative with regard to every significant story that they deem worthy of reporting, and their biases also impact the question of *which* stories are reported and presented to the public, and which storis are ignored completely. If you know, for example, the *races* of the police officers and the suspects involved in any arrests culminating in death or bodily harm to the suspect, then you can be *very* confident about whether the event will or will not receive any attention from the "mainstream" media. All other facts pertaining to the case in question will be treated as if they are irrelevant and unworthy of public consumption. If a corporation is accused of some form of malfeasance, just check to see which of the major political parties tends to receive the lion's share of contributions from the company in question, and you can reliably predict the degree of attention the allegation will garner from the usual suspect media outlets. At some point the "news" became nothing more than political propaganda. Really, there is almost no point in watching *any* of it anymore. So, *stop* doing so. Find a better way to spend your time.

April 7, 2021

When and why did hardtack go out of style as a long-life survival food? The standard recipe is fairly simple and straightforward, the resulting product remains edible for longer than the typical length of a human life, it requires very little by way of special storage conditions, and it is one of least expensive foods that does not grow directly out of the ground in your backyard. Admittedly, hardtack is not exactly rich in nutrients, but it *is* quite filling and substantial. Also, while it is not particularly tasty, consuming it is generally preferable to slow, painful starvation. A bit of peanut butter, jam, or hazelnut spread on top renders hardtack far more pleasing to the palate, and it can be dipped into soup, hummus, or cream cheese to enhance the flavor profile somewhat. The most salient feature of hardtack is that, for all intents and purposes, the stuff *never* goes bad. You have read about soldiers fighting in the Spanish-American war consuming hardtack that was originally manufactured for soldiers fighting in the United States Civil War. Rumor has it that the same Civil War batch survived long enough to be used by Americans fighting in World War I. *That* is a superfood. You can still purchase hardtack today, but almost no one talks about it or demonstrates a proper appreciation of this minor culinary miracle. Survivalists and "preppers" seem to be the last hardtack afficionados. That is all well and good. Those who appreciate the past are also those most likely to survive the coming collapse of the global supply chain. Lowly hardtack may prove to be a source of salvation in the not-too-distant future. You must admit a certain satisfaction that you derive from imagining all the people who think that they need the most expensive types of gourmet food begging, someday, from those who have learned to value hardtack, lentils, and vegetables they grow in the backyard. Oh, what a *wonderful* (and *just*) world that would be.

April 8, 2021

In certain areas of the nation, the lockdown rules continue to be enforced, whereas other areas have been largely or entirely opened back up for economic and social transactions for some time now. It does not trouble you to confess that you really have *no* idea whether, or to what extent, any of the lockdown and social distancing measures were necessary, or whether they saved more lives than they cost. It is fairly clear that some number of lives lost are attributable to suicide, drug overdoses, and missed medical appointments that, at least arguably, would not have happened under more usual circumstances. Then again, it is very plausible that more transmission of the virus, and presumably a greater number of deaths and hospitalizations would have occurred if interactions would have stayed "usual" in the areas of economic and social commerce. So, there are too many unknown, and possibly *unknowable*, variables for you to develop much of an assessment of the positive and negative consequences of the lockdowns as compared with the absence of those measures. To put the matter simply, you have no idea whether political leadership at the federal and state levels have *saved* many lives, *cost* many lives, destroyed the economy without justification, or simply taken steps that needed to be taken. One thing about which you *are* fairly confident, however, is that most of the people in positions of political power derived a disturbing degree of personal *pleasure* from this period of relatively unbridled authoritarianism. People who *seek* power over others are *never* to be trusted with it.

Something of a paradox, is it not?

April 9, 2021

Another celebrity is revealed to be a predatory pedophile, and the nation responds with a collective yawn and shrug. You are willing to wager that this person will face no *earthly* punishment for the vile depravity in question. Indeed, the societal abasement has reached the point at which you would not be the least bit surprised to see and hear this miscreant applauded for the repugnant behavior in question. The most shockingly despicable conduct is *not* very gradually becoming common and normalized all across the culture by which you find yourself surrounded. Even murderers in prison for the remainder of their lives will not tolerate child molesters in their midst, but pedophiles are permitted to move among us, and allowed to attempt to prey upon our children, and this is countenanced for reasons that you simply cannot understand. Indeed, you do not know that you have encountered any actual reasons or any actual argument to justify allowing pedophiles to exist anywhere *other* than prisons. These creatures draw breath, and precisely *nothing* about the world is thereby improved. They are the most prolific of all violent criminals, they are the least likely to be rehabilitated or reformed, and their victims are more likely to recapitulate the behavior to which they have been subjected than are the victims of *any* other violent crime. The wisest method of managing this problem is about as obvious as is possible, and it is also precluded by law. Humans, it turns out, are just not very good at governing themselves or their societies.

April 10, 2021

Watching the cage fights this afternoon, you could not help but notice something like the experience of *mourning*. It did not take a great deal of introspection to realize that you were grieving at the sight of young men doing things that you are *clearly* too old to do now, and that you were probably never tough enough or skilled enough to have done even in the flower of your youth. The ache in your back that you felt every time you shifted position on the couch was a not-so-gentle reminder that you are now well into the downhill slide of the latter half of your time on this planet. Watching young, athletic men of steel just reinforces your own experience of physical decline. Perhaps there are also pangs of mortality mixed in with the feelings of age-induced inadequacy, but the prospect of your own death has never really held any particular dread for you, unless you are deeply self-deceived about the matter. You would prefer to die younger if only it meant that you could remain strong, healthy, and unimpeded by injury right up until the moment of your "untimely" death. The years that remain for you, if indeed you *have* years left remaining to you, are bound to be besotted by the maladies and depreciation that seem inevitably to attend old age. This is no reason to complain or to shake your fist at God, but you would be lying to yourself if you claimed that getting old does not bother you in the *least*. It is, thus far, preferable to the alternative. With that faint praise, you may have offered the entirety of the advantages of aging. Some say wisdom comes with years. You, however, have not noticed this in your own case.

April 11, 2021

Once again, it seems that your stupid cat has gotten the better of you. After waking you up *far* too early this morning, he managed to get you to feed him, clean out his litter box, and scratch him behind the ears and under his chin, before retiring to your bed for the remainder of the day. Legally, you *own* him, but it is sometimes difficult to shake the feeling that the cat is not-so-secretly in charge, and that he knows this at some rudimentary level. His morning "Meow!" has a summoning quality to it. You do not experience it so much as a plaintive *request* for services, but rather more like a *command*. He seems genuinely irritated when you fail to respond with sufficient urgency, and if you did not know better, you could swear that he sometimes looks as if he is considering terminating your employment with the firm. The cat is an imperious creature, though he has done precisely *nothing* to earn his supervisory position. At some level, you have accepted that you are part of his staff, and you long for the days when you also had a dog around the house to maintain some semblance of a balance of power. The dog *knew* that you were in charge. The dog *liked* it that way. The dog also *hated* the cat (as God intended), and stood athwart all feline attempts to lord it over the household. The dog understood nature's hierarchy. The cat, on the other hand, has no respect for the creatures with the opposable thumbs. He remains unimpressed. When it is time to put the cat to sleep, you will perform your final task on his behalf. It will be something of a shame. For all his faults, he is still *your* kitty. You get the feeling *he* sees the matter differently.

April 12, 2021

The advocates of irrational "tolerance" are, once again, defending the indefensible rather than simply calling out vile, despicable behavior and pronouncing it *evil*. This practice of dressing vice and cowardice up as virtue has become so commonplace that you have begun to wonder whether the public at large can still distinguish phony virtue *signaling* from actual virtuous conduct. There is, obviously, nothing virtuous about *tolerating* the systematic abuse and miseducation of yet another generation of children who will grow up to be misinformed citizens and incompetent professionals in one field or another. It is already something of a rarity to hear anyone under the age of thirty talking sense about any societal, cultural, or political issue. There was a time when it was merely the *vast* majority of "educators" who spent nearly all of their waking hours *lying* to impressionable young people. Today, corporations and professional media talking heads have joined in on the prevaricating. Offering up the lie *de jour* has been adopted as standard practice by the intelligence community, the top military brass, medical doctors, and even large numbers of those who call themselves clergy. You now inhabit the *culture of the lie*, and you move among people who are more interested in hearing comforting nonsense than they have ever been interested in pursuing the truth. It seems that a culture with such defects cannot long persist, or so you may, at least, *hope*. Do not even *sigh* when the collapse comes. A *chuckle* would be more appropriate.

April 13, 2021

After several years of consideration, you have come to the conclusion that we are all faced with something like a strict disjunction. Either God exists, or there is no such thing as objective, absolute moral fact. It is, in a manner of speaking, *divine command theory* or it is *nothing*. Utilitarianism, Kantian deontology, Aristotelian natural theory, and other attempts to identify a groundwork for objective morality have proven to be abject failures. In the absence of a Creator with the legitimate authority to issue universal commands concerning good and evil, there is simply nothing else that can plausibly distinguish the good from the evil in a manner that is both *binding* and unconditional. Certainly nothing that humans construct, and nothing about human desires or satisfaction is invariant, universal, or immutable. The sources from which persons and cultures derive pleasure vary from time to time, place to place, and person to person. Human reason is not much more promising as a repository of objective moral fact. Your species is deeply flawed, limited, and not remotely authorized to impose binding moral constraints upon members of the biological type. In other words, no one *needs* to care what other people *regard* as good or evil. The natural world is obviously devoid of morality entirely. Lions *kill* prey, but they do not commit *murder*. If there is no God who issues an injunction prohibiting murder, then the same that is true of other predators is also true of predatory human beings. They *kill* other people when it suits them to do so, but *murder* is supposed to be *inherently* illegitimate and unjustifiable. If there is no Creator and Designer to whom we all owe the debt of our very existence, then there is no moral prohibition to which we are compelled to adhere or from which we are obliged to suffer the consequences of the Creator's inerrant moral judgement. If murder is not evil *because God makes it so*, then murder is not *actually evil* at all. It may be hideous, terrifying, repugnant, deleterious to society at large, and it may be defective in many other ways as well. Murder, however, like every other sin, is only *evil* if there is a God to *make* it so. If there is *no* God, then all talk of "morality" is nothing more than clumsy attempts at social engineering and propaganda. If the "engineers" are merely human, then *why* would you be *obligated* to obey? *They* did not *design* you. They are nothing more than talking apes.

April 14, 2021

People who habitually and reflexively make excuses for their misbehavior and terrible decisions are, in nearly every case, doomed to lives *devoid* of flourishing or virtue. The excuses foreclose any honest evaluation of the root causes for nearly all of their difficulties, and people in positions of power and influence will *always* aid and abet any form of stupidity or dishonesty that keeps the broader public in a position of dependency and subservience. In other words, people in power have taught and encouraged the powerless to blame their travails on circumstances beyond their control, and the powerless prefer to blame their powerlessness on "the system," rather than taking responsibility for their own irrational decisions and deleterious patterns of behavior. Those in power then offer the powerless just enough help by way of social programs and welfare (by various other names) to keep the poor alive and voting for the politicians who tell them that their poverty is not their fault, and that their survival depends upon continuing to support the very "system" that allegedly "keeps them down" by convincing them that they lack the capacity to lift themselves out of destitution and powerlessness. So, in a perverse sense, those who blame "the system" for their travails are partially *correct*. Of course, they are only correct because they are stupid, weak, and easily manipulated by the people who feed on their dependency. This will *not* end well. Of course, most *endings*, outside of Hollywood movies, are not particularly happy. They mostly involve *death*.

April 15, 2021

The culture of the lie reasserts itself *daily*, if not even more frequently than that. Almost no one in the public sphere dares tell the truth about what they really believe, what they really value, or what they really think of the other talking apes. Everyone staggers around pretending to have no biases, or at least none that genuinely impact their dealings with others, and phony reverence is paid to persons whom not a soul has *ever* respected or regarded as heroic or noble in the *least*. Some of the most despicable human beings ever to befoul the face of your planet are treated as if they warrant the worship of the unwashed masses. Each day, a new "hero" is invented out of whole cloth, and a *real* hero is dragged through the rhetorical mud for the "sin" of having lived a century or more before the current crop of dimwitted primates, and also having believed what *everyone* else of his day believed. So many imbeciles are utterly convinced of their moral and intellectual superiority to figures such as Aristotle, Newton, and Aquinas that these great minds might be removed from the histories and from our collective, cultural memories by idiots who have never read a word that any of them have written, and certainly could not grasp even the most fundamental concepts with which these intellectual giants struggled manfully. The liars, the morons, and the cowards now run nearly the entirety of the Western World, and for this reason the West teeters on the brink of extinction. This too, it seems, shall pass away. The worthless will see to it. Can *no one* take a *joke* anymore?

April 16, 2021

The hypocrisy of Marxists making millions of dollars by exploiting the poor, purchasing mansions for themselves and their family members, and continuing to shout Marxist rhetoric about the proletariat is simply *priceless*. Of course, the absence of prices is probably a welcome consequence from a (phony) Marxist perspective, but those mansions *do* come at a *price*, do they not? People who reject the phenomenon of private property while gobbling up property for their *private* use and control are simply the most ludicrous human beings on the planet today. That title, by the way, is particularly impressive given the astonishing number of ludicrous people currently polluting every nation and culture across the Western World. There are, of course, more than enough ridiculous,

hypocrites the world over,
but it seems that there is
some form of special
acceleration among members of
this "demographic" in the
West. Hypocrisy takes *many*
different forms, and it is
distributed *across* the socio-
political continuum, as well
as it is spread across all
religious groups – to say
nothing of atheists and
secularists. Indeed, nearly
everyone indulges in the
occasional act of hypocrisy,
as nearly all of us
occasionally do things
against which we have
inveighed at one time or
another. Nonetheless, it is
very clear that one
particular segment of the
socio-political sphere is, at
this moment in history, *far*
more hypocritical than any
competitor class. The fact
that they decline even to
attempt to fake sincerity is,
arguably, the only honest
thing about these charlatans.
How are they *not* dressed as

clowns? How are they not being dragged to public squares for beatings along with tar and feathering? They are literally the *worst* people on the planet. Yet, somehow, they are treated as if their words matter. This is simply baffling. *Where* is the punchline?

April 17, 2021

The citizens of your nation no longer enjoy a collective, common sense of what constitutes a reasonable belief and respectable conduct. On a daily basis, you witness public behavior that would have resulted in ostracism, at the very least, and beatings not so very long ago. Such beatings would not, have merited any such thing as an investigation beyond some cursory survey of the readily-observable data. Any pedophile caught in the act, or *describing* an act of child molestation, would have been beaten unceremoniously to death, or as near to it as could be managed in the time and space permitted, and not *one* human being would have objected in the least. No trial would have been necessary for the pedophile, and any trial of those administering "justice" in the matter would have resulted in a not guilty verdict. No one would have expressed the *slightest* sympathy for the deviant predator. Today, people gather at libraries where "parents" *watch* pedophiles grooming their children to be victimized even more thoroughly at some later time. Somehow, *no* blood is shed at events of this nature. *That* is, perhaps, the greatest tragedy pertaining to this new expression of perversion and depravity. No one savages these bastards. What kind of father would sit by and allow that type of behavior involving his own child? What can *any* of the participants in these events *possibly* be thinking? If this is what the future holds, then let the future be cleansed by hellfire. Sometimes, a shrug is *not* the best you can manage. Sometimes a mere shrug is a *sin*.

April 18, 2021

The world has always been filled with injustice, tyranny, and oppression. History is *replete* with genocide, warfare, slavery, and slaughter by just about any means imaginable. The injustice you find "in your neighborhood" is as nothing compared to most standards that may be found throughout the ages and across much of the planet even today. You live in a nation in which suicide is typically *more* common than homicide. How it can be that so many people choose to destroy *themselves* rather than directing the lethality at others is a phenomenon that you find intriguing. Sure, many suicides do plenty of damage to others in the years before they finally decide to do themselves in, but the *coup de grace* is, in most cases reserved for the *self*. That is more than just a little bit odd, is it not? Despite all of the complaining about various forms of mistreatment, deprivation, encroachment upon rights and liberties, more people choose to remove *themselves* from the field upon which life is "played" than choose to attempt to remove others from the game. Has *that* always been so? Did your prehistoric ancestors commit suicide? If so, then was such a thing a very *rare* occurrence, or was it as proportionally commonplace as it is in the time and place that you inhabit? No, something must have changed on the *inside* of the human animal. It seems that a void is widening inside of, for lack of a better term, the human *soul*. An awful lot of people appear to be sick of themselves. That is probably an oversimplification. Nothing follows about the observation being *untrue*.

April 19, 2021

There are not, as it turns out, two sides to *every* story. Sometimes, nothing approaching a *reasonable* disagreement is to be had. Disagreements will still occur when only *one* side has a leg upon which to stand, but only pseudo-debate can issue from exchanges concerning such matters. If you encounter someone who claims to believe that the moon really *is* made of green cheese, then you can safely conclude that you are dealing with a lunatic or a liar. No *rational* adult actually believes any such thing. The same can, of course, be said about claims that, somehow, get bandied about as if they are *not* as *ludicrous* as the claim that the moon is made of green cheese. There are people who pretend to believe that biology does *not* determine sex, for example. Of course, *no* rational adult *actually* believes any such thing (protestations to the contrary notwithstanding). Why, then, are there so many educated persons who are willing to assert this kind of nonsense in public, and why do they not pay an immediate price for giving voice to such gibberish – a price on the order of the price paid by the liars and dimwits who say that the moon is made of cheese? How are *any* of these charlatans ever employable for the remainder of their lives? How are they *not* relegated to lives of infamy and shame? It is all something of a mystery. Evidently, a society can succumb to mental illness much as can an individual member of that society. It is a bizarre thing to observe. Lunacy spreads like a viral pandemic. No vaccination will forestall the consequences. Try not to take any of this idiocy too seriously.

April 20, 2021

Dead bodies that have spent a few years or a few decades in the ground all look more or less the same. The size varies a bit, and morphology is a little different from one body to another, but the untrained eye cannot discern very much about the life that was lived before the body expired. This is interesting given that the lives lived within these animated bodies, before the light goes out, are strikingly different in their particulars. Some live lives of material luxury and terrestrial power, whereas others live in poverty, powerlessness, and anonymity. Most of those who read *this* book are living lives somewhere between the extremes just described. People are alive on this planet for seven or eight decades, in the average instance, and then their bodies turn to dust, ashes, and worm food. For some reason, most of us have the feeling that there is something like a meaning or a purpose to the things we do before we end up in the ground. Is this, perhaps, an evolutionary adaptation of some kind? Did those of our ancestors who sought purpose tend to live long enough to procreate, while those who lacked the feeling of purpose did not survive as long? If so, the survival advantage to experiencing life as if it is meaningful is less than *obvious*. It is *possible*, is it not, that the *feeling* of meaning, the *appearance* of purpose, is more than *merely* apparent? Suppose, just for the sake of argument, that your life *has* meaning, and that your presence here on this planet *is* directed toward some goal or purpose of which you are only dimly aware and that no one can conclusively demonstrate beyond a reasonable doubt.

Suppose, in other words, that you are here for a *reason*. Suppose that the reason is not yours to *choose*, but is rather yours to *discover*. You only get so much time to figure out what you are supposed to be doing. When your time is up, you go in the ground, and you end up being mostly indistinguishable from the other dead bodies that lie in the dirt. Be careful about wasting your time. In the end, you really do not have much else. Maybe God loves to give us puzzles. Maybe we invent them for ourselves. Either way, it is wise to learn to respect a good puzzle.

April 21, 2021

You can do as you wish, and you can do so with a clear conscience, but *only* if your wishes are morally permissible and untainted by vice. For most people, that last bit is the rub. Human desires, if they are not guided by reason or by some reliably virtuous wellspring, tend to be both selfish and self-destructive (not to mention detrimental to the interests of others with whom the self tends to interact). It is worth noting that when humans are left to their own devices, the result is generally self-abasement and some form of depravity or other that damages those with whom they come into contact. If you did not know better, you could swear that humanity suffers from a *bestial* nature. Indeed, you do *not* "know better" at all. It is not the least bit surprising or inappropriate that so many

Christians describe human nature as inherently "fallen." This might be the single most apt description of the people whom you encounter every day, as well as the person you encounter in the mirror. The whole lot of you appear to have no idea what to do with yourselves (or what to *avoid* doing) unless you believe that someone is watching over you with lash in hand. Anyone claiming that "people are basically good" has clearly never spent much time paying *attention* to the things that people say and do. People are basically a *mess*. *You* are one of them. Arrogance and self-satisfaction among the talking primates seem almost laughable. The whole phenomenon of the human race is *almost* a shame. Somewhere, there is good joke in all of this. The joke appears to be on *you*. Laughter seems *almost* appropriate. Then again, you

might be better off just
looking away.

April 22, 2021

Every once in a great (or not-so-great) while, it is useful and instructive to go at least one day without saying a word to anyone. You will probably notice the impulse to speak arising repeatedly throughout your silent period, and you will probably discern something of *what* you would have said had you not stopped yourself from speaking. Pay attention to how much of what you almost said would actually have been *worth* saying. The probability that *most* of what you were going to say did not *need* to be said is *very* high. All too often the talking primates do their speaking not for the sake of transmitting some form of valuable information, but rather they make noises with their faces because it is the most reliable method to garner attention, or because it is the simplest way to dispel the awkward experience of prolonged silence in the company of the other talking apes. *Why* silence among the blathering primates should be unbearably cumbersome is something of a mystery, but it is clear that most of God's creatures who find that they are endowed with the gift of speech feel compelled to deploy that gift far, *far* too often. You have long known that you learn more from listening and observing than you will ever learn from running your mouth, but you keep talking without sufficient justification for doing so. This is a bad habit. It is no *less* bad merely because it is such a *common* habit. Shut up for a little while and see what you learn from the experience. If you learn something valuable, then shut up more frequently in the future. Humanity at large would suffer far less if it just spent less time and energy yapping. Some claim that silence is "golden," but it is probably better described as "reverent," and it is certainly much simpler and much more peaceful than is the incessant yammering in which so many seem to choose to engage. The first step to separating yourself from the beast that is the mob is to *stop* talking so much. It is much easier to walk away when you are *not* in the middle of a sentence.

April 23, 2021

The amount of self-inflicted suffering, failure, and dependency is ever on the increase in the society by which you are surrounded. If you did not know better, then you would probably be convinced that most of the "downtrodden" of your nation prefer a dismal, excruciating existence to the fairly readily-available access to various mechanisms of fairly reliable personal material advancement. People who simply finish high school (which, it is worth pointing out, is available for *free*), and refrain from producing offspring *before* getting married, are statistically *very* unlikely to lead lives filled with grinding poverty, repeated trips to prison, and relentlessly disastrous interpersonal relationships. To be sure, there are plenty of people who graduate high school and wait for marriage to make babies, but manage to "enjoy" disastrous marriages and other relationships nonetheless. They are, regrettably, not terribly difficult to find. Things can and do go wrong for folks from *every* walk of life, and from nearly every conceivable behavioral inclination. The probabilities of living through one emergency, disaster, and tragedy after another, however, decline markedly for people who simply make *rational* decisions. A mind *is*, indeed, a terrible thing to waste and, having wasted it, the remainder of the life lived in the absence of a functioning mind is mostly not worth having. Stupid people tend to suffer a great deal. This is, of course, not exactly an *injustice* so much as it is something like a manifestation of the laws of nature. Gravity causes things to crash to the ground.

Stupidity does *more* damage than that.

April 24, 2021

Consider the possibility that freedom is, paradoxical though this may seem, submission to God's will. For those who are disinclined to embrace belief in God, think of the *Tao* of Eastern philosophy as the force with which it is necessary to find harmony if you are going to experience anything like freedom *from* the control of governments, corporations, and other collectives of mere humans and their making. All of their propaganda, and all of their desperate efforts to manipulate your beliefs and your desires will not countervail against a commitment to find your place in God's plan, or to find your way of blending into the flow of events as governed by the natural *way of things*. God and the world are far larger, far older, and far more powerful than all human endeavor and edifice amalgamated together. Protagoras declared man to be the "measure of all things," but he was clearly *wrong* in this pronouncement. The world was here *long* before mankind showed up on the scene, and the earliest humans had to secure their survival by *obeying* nature's laws. If God is real, then God existed before *anything* else, and even the natural world and its laws must conform to His commands. Collections of human beings are collections of mere beasts with larger brains than the other animals. Mankind will never amount to more than that in its various groupings. An individual person, however, can rise above the tyranny of the masses through submission to the higher powers against which all lesser beings exist as mere playthings. *Never* obey the mob. They are spoiled children. Obey the *source* that gives birth to all things. Therein lies your freedom.

April 25, 2021

Government is a blunt instrument with which politicians claim to be able to perform delicate socio-economic surgery. They imply that they can engineer something approaching a utopian society while they indulge openly in corruption, stupidity, and utterly incompetent attempts to engineer their own extramarital affairs. So, a bunch of club-wielding dimwits claim that they are going to improve *your* life and your circumstances if only grant them the power to legislate and execute law and policy. Of course, the promises issued during political campaigns are worth *less* than the paper upon which they are *not* written. The candidates lie to the voters, the voters are (for the most part) well aware that the candidates are lying, but the voters cast their ballots for their preferred prevaricators nonetheless, because they believe that doing so is part of discharging their duties to the public at large. Either that or the voters simply have *no* idea what else to do about the pathetic and rapidly deteriorating state of the republic. In fact, no vote is *ever* going to improve anything that matters. The people *are* the problem. The system is *representative*. Thus, the problem elects a ruling class that exacerbates the problem. The cycle repeats every few years. In this manner, the republic commits suicide. Perhaps it is a type of justice after all. It is no tragedy when a nation of imbeciles gets exactly what it deserves. What do *you* care for such nonsense? Imbeciles are bound to dangle. There is *plenty* of rope. Actually, there is *exactly enough* of it.

April 26, 2021

A strange combination of conditions obtains these days. Everything about the nation in which you live and the culture in which you find yourself immersed is hysterical (in *both* senses), but *joking* about the lunacy appears to be prohibited. If you make fun of persons and events that simply *cry out* for ridicule, then your career will be jeopardized and your family may be endangered. Famous people say things in public that can only be uttered (non-ironically) by a maniac or a pathological liar, but if you point out the insanity and dishonesty, then *you* are the one who will be punished. The maniacal deceivers will be *celebrated*. Confronted with these states of affairs, despair is tempting, but it is also pointless, impotent, and pathetic. You must either risk the slings and arrows that are bound to follow when you tell the truth, or you must remain silent. It is difficult to determine which is the wiser or more virtuous course of action. If you risked only *yourself* and *your* interests, then it would be easy enough to choose the path of vocal resistance to the corruption and insanity. Given that the people you love may be placed at risk, however, the discretion of silence might be the better choice. You are not, after all, going to alter the course of cultural trajectory by speaking the truth to people who have no interest in hearing the truth. Perhaps quietly *watching* the disintegration all around you is the best option to which you have access. Indeed, you might want to become a hermit. Surely, the family will not object, right?

April 27, 2021

Country (the *real* stuff) music is largely about heartbreak, poverty, and death. Along with the *blues*, this makes country the most honest music you are likely to find. The kind of popular music that you hear on the radio or find in music videos is mostly designed to appeal to vapid, shallow teenagers who have no idea what really matters, and who have not yet had the opportunity to be beaten down and worn out by the real world. Young people are, with relatively rare exceptions, *stupid*. They are not entirely to blame for this condition, because older people have become too cowardly to teach young people the lessons they need most desperately to learn. Parents, all too often, allow their children to lead entirely parasitic lives for much, *much* longer than is required by nature. A fourteen-month-old child is incapable of contributing to the health and wellbeing of the family in any significant fashion. A fourteen-*year*-old child, however, is perfectly capable of working around the home, learning to cook and chop wood, and pursuing an education without suffering because of the requisite efforts. Do you remember getting fatigued when you were a teenager? It was nearly impossible for you to get tired, was it not? Today's youth are mostly soft, fat, lazy, weak, and emotionally stunted. Their parents and the surrounding culture are to blame for this condition. Young people are as pathetic as adults *allow* them to be. The kids will keep playing video games and inhabiting virtual reality until *actual* reality cannot compete for their attention. Thus, the road is paved with *no* intentions. Getting what

we deserve is going to be
ugly. Stock up on ammo.

April 28, 2021

Unlike the rest of God's creatures, people can speak. Therein lies the great majority of the problem. If the humans could only make hand gestures, or if they could only communicate via blinking in Morse Code, then most of them would be mostly tolerable (though *some* would surely manage to be irritating no matter what their limitations). It is worth noting, however, that getting angry at the humans has seldom, if ever, done you any *good*. When is the last time you caught yourself thinking, "Well, I sure am glad I blew my top a few minutes ago," and later bragging to others about all of the wonders you have accomplished while in a condition of sustained rage? Perhaps you managed an instance of self-defense while enraged, but could you not have defended yourself at least as successfully *without* losing your temper. Indeed, you are far more likely to experience some form of bodily *dysfunction* or other when you are under the influence of adrenaline and the other "fight or flight" chemicals. Consider your experience in combat sports when you were able to remain calm and composed compared to those occasions when you allowed your temper to get the better of you. Professional boxing and mixed martial arts trainers work very hard to keep their fighters *reasoning* between rounds. So, conduct yourself like a well-trained professional fighter, and do *not* lose your cool. You will never regret a moment of reasonable equanimity.

April 29, 2021

Pay no attention to the constant blather and bleating of phony outrage constantly screaming from every media orifice. A rational person does not indulge in the quixotic endeavor of attempting to speak sense to liars who have not the slightest interest in evidence, rationality, or the pursuit of truth. Those who can only communicate by *performing*, by *pretending* to believe things that *no one* believes, and by *acting* like they are horrified by events that are not even slightly frightening to *any* adult, are properly treated as petulant children, and their constant complaints are properly regarded as meaningless noise and nothing more. Do not expect any words that you might utter or type to have the slightest impact on these various performances. Also, *never* lose sight of the fact that they are merely performing, and *none* of these people actually believe *any* of the nonsense they spout. If you watch their behavior when they are not engaged in dishonest debate, then you will readily discern their actual beliefs and values. Your eyes inform you much more reliably than do your ears when it comes to the project of figuring out what another person really thinks about the nature of reality. If a person claims not to believe in gravity, then check which direction he looks when he drops something. If he looks down (and he *will*), then you can safely chalk up his denial of gravity to dishonesty. You can also dismiss him from your company. It is better to enjoy solitude than to tolerate a lying companion.

April 30, 2021

The appearance of design in the natural world cries out for explanation. Either it appears to have been designed to permit intelligent, complex living beings because it *was* designed for this purpose (and possibly others), or it *merely* appears to have been designed though it was *not*. Why should any special burden of proof fall on those who claim that a thing *is* what it *appears to be*? Of course, mere appearance, in and of itself, does not *prove* that what appears to be so, upon careful analysis, will be the discovered *reality*. There *are* some stubbornly persistent illusions. Why, however, should anyone believe that apparent fine-tuning of the various universal constants will prove to be *merely* apparent upon careful inspection? At the moment, the best alternative hypothesis seems to involve an infinite, or enormously fecund multiverse as a means of explaining the apparently miniscule probability that there should exist an anthropic universe, and that we should exist so as to puzzle about the matter. As for the (alleged) evidence that such a multiverse actually exists, can anyone honestly claim that it is more compelling than the apparent evidence of design? Apart from desperation to avoid the inference to a Designer, what reason is there to place your *faith* in a multiverse? There is certainly no *proof* that it exists. If the choice is God or Multiverse, then the former option has, at the very least, the virtue of an existing narrative. Devotees of the latter appear to be, more or less, just making it up as they go along.

May 1, 2021

Today is "Commie Christmas." That, all by itself, is sufficient reason to remain skeptical about the future of the human race. There are, evidently, people who are so dense, so poorly informed, or so perverse, that they actually celebrate an ideology that resulted in the slaughter of approximately one hundred million innocent people at the hands of their *own* governments. Apart from that, communism also appears to have been designed for ants or lemmings rather than for reasoning beings. Of course, most human communists seem to keep their reasoning to a minimum – at least where socio-political matters are concerned. Most of them seem not to notice that they are practicing a secularized religion in which the *State*, or the *Collective* (here properly capitalized) stands in for the God of the

Abrahamic religions. They submit themselves to the will of the Collective, and to the wisdom of its governing Overlords, in much the same way that Muslims are expected to submit and surrender to the will of Allah. In the case of the *theistic* religions, there is, at the very least, a potential afterlife and the hope of God's grace for one's faith and works. Communism offers only subjugation and the closest approximation to equal *misery* that an assemblage of vaguely psychotic talking apes can manage. Yes, what is *not* to celebrate about the proletariat rising to dictatorship? One wonders, however, *who* will be *taking* the "dictation" in the world to come. Thus always with egalitarians, is it not? Oh, happy day.

May 2, 2021

There *are* ugly babies. You have *seen* them. There *are* stupid ideas. You have *heard* and read them articulated. While you recognize that there is probably no moral justification for pointing out a hideous infant, there are lots of reasons to point out stupid ideas, *if* you intend to continue to live in any type of community involving other persons. In your case, this particular "if" seems to gain urgency and salience with each passing year (if not each passing *day*). Do you *really* need to keep associating with the kinds of morons who believe that socialism is a viable system for distributing and managing goods and the means of producing goods? All attempts to reason with these people are hopeless or, at the very least, not worth the time and effort you would need to expend. Why not just allow those who cannot learn the blindingly obvious lessons of history suffer the fate of repeating the same mistakes that plagued the 20th Century? It is not as if your efforts are likely to forestall the consequences of mass stupidity conjoined with the blunderbuss that is democracy. The moron majority is bound to have its way. You are best served by doing everything in your power to remain as insulated as possible from the inevitable fallout of expanding government "assistance" in lives of the populace. Store up food, water, ammo, and move to a small town. Once there, live quietly in a manner that will attract as little attention as possible. Having done that, sit back and watch the "ugly babies" of socialism and moral nihilism wreak their usual havoc. It should be an

interesting train wreck. Just
stay off of the tracks.

May 3, 2021

When did it become unfashionable to point out persons in positions of power and influence who are also morally reprehensible louts? How is it that occupying the Governor's mansion is supposed to serve as insulation from criticism concerning one's marital fidelity (or lack thereof), for example? If your Governor, Senator, or Congressional Representative is an adulterer, and a *lot* of them are, then you certainly have no moral obligation to refrain from mentioning this particular character flaw, and a case can be made that you are obligated actively to bring this to the attention of voters and other citizens who may not yet be aware of the peccadillo in question. Do not make the mistake of assuming that you are morally superior to the person in question merely because you are not guilty of this *particular* sin. Passing judgement is not, in and of itself, inherently problematic, but it is the tendency to fail to judge *yourself* and *your* actions by the same standards to which you tend to subject others that constitutes *hypocrisy*. Speaking of which, how is it that so many people in positions of power are also inveterate hypocrites? Perhaps the voters have become comfortable with hypocrisy because they encounter it so frequently in *themselves*. They *are* choosing *representatives*, are they not? This may be the reason that so many people have become so timorous in public discourse. They know how easily criticism can be directed at *their* character and behavior. A nation of terrible people inevitably becomes a terrible nation. Do you have a *better* explanation

for the current state of
"your" nation?

May 4, 2021

Seeing things that you prefer not to have seen, hearing words that you would rather not have heard, and experiencing facets of the human condition about which no one can possibly be particularly proud, these *may* constitute *misfortunes* of a sort. You would do well to remember, however, that these unpleasant experiences can only befall you because you have had the great good fortune to *exist*, and to appear on the scene in the form of a (sometimes) reasoning being with the cognitive wherewithal to interrogate the value of your experiences. In other words, any internal complaint that arises within your unruly consciousness should be tempered and dampened by the foreknowledge that the universe could have made do *without* you. Do you see people behaving in abominable fashion and doing things to their fellow human beings that ought *never* to be done to anyone? It certainly seems that way. You would prefer that genocide, rape, and oppression did *not* occur. You would prefer that no one ever even *considered* perpetrating such atrocities. Would you, however, prefer that *you* did not exist so that you could not encounter this feature of reality, or would you prefer that *no* intelligent beings ever existed anywhere? It seems that you can imagine untold preferable possible worlds. It also seems that you can imagine innumerably many worlds in which *nothing* significant ever happens. You can stamp your feet and demand that the world must conform to your whims. Try it. How did *that* work out? The world as it *might have been*, is not the world as it, in fact, *is*. Try to avoid getting worked up about worlds that *you* do *not* inhabit.

May 5, 2021

It seems that anxiety and depression have attained epidemic proportions across the modern West. These conditions may be equally prevalent in other regions and cultures as well, but you live in the West, and your experience is centered in the place you live. It is probably best to write about what you *know and have experienced*, after all. All things considered, you are inclined to a sympathetic assessment of the very common experience of anxiety and depression given the current state of the contemporary West and the culture (or *cultures*) found there. Indeed, much of the "mainstream" media seem to be devoted to the project of *keeping* the public in a condition of constant, relentless terror and worry. The media tell the public that the environment is on the brink of collapse, the various military powers are always about to escalate active warfare activities, the "powers that be" always endeavor to manipulate the people into unhealthy and unwise behaviors, and all of this is coupled with the implicit message that there is no God watching or governing the unfolding of events. The public is told, "Everything that matters is going very, very badly, and help is *not* on the way." That message, by the way, might be quite accurate (or it might not). Given the ubiquity of that narrative, however, it is simply not surprising that vast swathes of the public fall into despair. Of course, it does not follow that *you* are excused for falling similarly into despondency. *You* are *not* the masses. Do not surrender to the forces that undermine the serenity of the crowd. Keep breathing

in and out. The world will
keep turning.

May 6, 2021

There are still plenty of areas in your vicinity, within driving distance if not also within *walking* distance, that are breathtakingly beautiful and fill you with an appreciation of the natural world that is, at least arguably, unmatched by anything that the humans have ever accomplished. What human work of art or architecture can hold a candle to the Grand Canyon? Any attempted comparison is unfair to the artists or architects and builders involved. Nature commands resources that no collection of talking primates could ever hope to control. The amount of time necessary to form the natural wonders is, at least in many cases, simply not fathomable by creatures who tend to live less than a century as individuals, and who have gathered in collectives about the surface of the planet for only thousands, tens of thousands, hundreds of thousands, or perhaps a handful of millions of years. What is the human race supposed to do that could possibly warrant comparison to the night sky? Against trillions of stars and galaxies, the collective product of *all* human endeavor stands no chance in the contest to capture the imaginations and garner the awe of those very humans themselves. You are a tiny, ephemeral, and insignificant element of one little blob of mud and water among trillions of other celestial bodies. In *your* honor, perhaps a *sandwich* shall be made. Maybe you will have chips as well. All things considered you really should *not* complain. Eat your lunch and get back to work on stuff that time is going to destroy and erase from the universe. Try to be a *good* talking ape. You might

even get a pickle spear with
your sandwich.

May 7, 2021

There *are* people who prefer to drink decaffeinated coffee, even in the morning. Those people are *wrong*. No, it is *not* merely a matter of preference or inclination. Those people are *morally* wrong. They are no better than people who eat sugarless chocolate (as if there could be a *point* to *that*), or people who go into a fast-food burger "restaurant" and order a *salad*. People who want salad have *no* business acquiring one in a place that *exists* for the purpose of producing and selling greasy, unhealthy, but tasty hamburgers and fries, along with soda or milkshakes to wash the culinary detritus down. The point of a "restaurant" that sells junk food is entirely incompatible with the maintenance of a *healthy* diet. If you want food that is *good for you*, then what in the world are you doing going to a place that specializes in delicious garbage accompanied by "placemats" emblazoned with cartoon characters, all of which is presented inside a building accompanied by a ridiculous mascot that towers about the roof? When in Rome, do *not* go to a fast-food place! You are in Rome, *Italy*! They have *real* food there. In any event, people who drink decaffeinated coffee should only be permitted to associate with those who drink non-alcoholic *beer*. There *are* other beverages without *booze* in them. Perhaps a *diet* soda would serve just as well. Those who *cannot* see their way to the *heart* of the matter are simply unfit company for anyone apart from each other. At least drug addicts *know* that they want *drugs*. No one ever got busted for possession of "diet" methamphetamine.

May 8, 2021

At some point, it becomes irrational and unhealthy to continue accepting the conditions and the relationships to which you have become accustomed. The very *idea* of governance is inherently displeasing, but you accept a certain degree of limitation upon your autonomy in exchange for avoiding chaos, anarchy, and a state of constant instability. At this particular moment in the history of "your" nation, however, the governing bodies at the federal, state, and local levels have become so corrupt, incompetent, and intrusive that you must consider the possibility that they are no longer worth the price you pay in taxes, legal restrictions upon your person and your conduct, or encroachments upon your privacy and your chosen forms of self-expression. In other words, it is not at all clear that national defense, interstate highways, and efficient indoor plumbing are sufficient compensation for the proliferation of petty martinets constantly telling you what you can and cannot do, where you can and cannot go, what you must and must not value, and screeching at you to feel guilty about the immutable biological condition in which you were *born*. If *they* (the big "they") *hate* you because of your race, sex, and sexual orientation, then *they* can get *bent*, and *you* have *no* obligation to embrace governance by people and institutions who have chosen to treat you as if you are a nuisance at best, and a congenital miscreant at worst (so far). You must continue to avoid falling afoul of the law and its mechanisms of punishment, but you should probably ignore the government apart from practical necessity. Government *hates* you and has nothing but contempt for people "like" you. It is almost always inadvisable to dance to the tune played by a piper who wants to rob you blind, drive you out of the dance hall, and then murder you in some dark alley. Leave all of that behind voluntarily and go make your own music elsewhere. You need not leave the country, but you may need to take leave of your *love* for it. Does this nation still *deserve* your affections? The answer does not come as easily as you may have hoped.

May 9, 2021

The "inner work" is more fundamental, more important, and more *difficult* than any endeavor involving the external world. Your mental states, your character, and your values are largely subject to your choices and your intellectual effort. You will have a very hard time accomplishing anything worthwhile in the spheres of interpersonal relationships, career, or contributions to society at large if you do not *first* rectify your *own* temperament. If you are inclined toward vice, then any virtue that springs from your actions and your efforts does so only fortuitously, and you will have earned neither praise nor any justified self-satisfaction for your deeds. Do not go through life as the type of person who must *hope* that your *true* motives will never be discovered. Discipline yourself to be able to behave exactly as you *like* while never doing *anything* unjust or otherwise blameworthy. Work on yourself until virtuous acts flow from you as naturally as does your native tongue. Much as you had to acquire the ability to speak a language, so too must you *acquire* the ability to behave in noble and admirable fashion without struggling against your more bestial impulses. Train yourself to respond to any and all circumstances and challenges with reason and decency. Do not allow your reflexive urges to determine your conduct. Remember that it is better to be a *good* person than it is to be a satiated beast. A pig happily cavorting in the mud, is a *swine* nonetheless. Surely, there is more to a well-lived human life than there is to the pursuits of a selfishly contented pig.

May 10, 2021

What kind of lunatic or dimwit would *ever* voluntarily give away an advantage? If you are in a position that provides you with some benefit that is unique or available only to a small subset of those concerned in the matter at hand, then you behave like a fool if you choose not to avail yourself of the benefit in question. For example, if you are running for political office and your campaign receives far more money in contributions than does your opponent, then you are engaged in political malpractice if you decline to spend the additional money in ways that help you win the election, or if you decide to donate enough of your campaign funds to your opponent so that the two of you have equivalent money to spend on the race. When you have the opportunity to be victorious in any contest, and the opportunity is acquired in honest and legally permissible fashion, you ought to press forward to victory, or simply drop out of the contest altogether. Do not hamstring *yourself* in any competitive endeavor while also calling yourself a *rational* adult. Play to win or do not play at all. The latter option is all too frequently treated as if it is not *really* available. You do not *have* to compete in *every* contest that presents itself for your consideration. Sometimes you are better off remaining out of the fray. When you have no viable choice but to compete, you are pathetic if you do not do your best to win. When an advantage falls into your lap, take hold of it and use it to the best of your ability. Never look the proverbial "gift horse in the mouth," and try to avoid future misuses of the term "proverbial." Move forward and do your best.

May 11, 2021

Most of what you say, and most of what you write will have *no* discernible impact on most of the people who hear or read it. This is partially attributable to the fact that most of what you have to say is just not all that important or insightful. Do not kid yourself about this. Try to avoid pretending that you serve as some kind of modern-day Oracle at Delphi. You are no such thing. Apollo has never said a *word* to you. The other thing that you ought to realize is that most people lack the capacity to assimilate the information you provide, and *very* few people are capable of translating anything that they may have learned into a viable plan of action. Trying to present and explain lessons about self-discipline and virtue to people who lack the capacity to understand those lessons, or to persons who lack the diligence to do anything useful with those lessons, is a lot like trying to teach dogs to climb trees. You *might* actually find one who can manage it, but even if you do, it will never be worth the time and effort required to pull off the accomplishment in question. Why should you care what other people do or do not understand, and why should you care how other people conduct themselves? Keep your eyes open, and try to step out of the way of cars speeding toward you, but apart from that kind of thing, you really need not concern yourself with what goes on in minds and bodies other than your own. You will only come to needless grief by trying to convince other people to think and act as you would prefer. It would be far better for you to rid yourself of any such preference. Stop caring about

the stuff you cannot control.
Serenity follows.

May 12, 2021

It looks as if a significant inflationary spike is on its way, and all indications (apart from assurances on the part of the Federal Reserve that no rational adult ought to take seriously) are pointing toward a protracted increase in prices on most consumer goods. In other words, all of the stuff that you need to buy in order to survive is going to cost a *lot* more for the foreseeable future. Luckily, you perceived this as a likely outcome of the ridiculous "government stimulus" response to the ongoing pandemic and the economic consequences thereof. The closets are filled with long shelf-life meat, fruits, grains, pasta, and vegetables should serve to hedge against the effects of the inflation that has already begun, and the continuing inflation that you expect to experience for several years to come (if not longer). Most of this food is not exactly *gourmet* or restaurant quality, but who the hell ever told you that you were *entitled* to enjoy exquisite taste in *all* of your meals. Fill your face with nutrition and remain thankful for the opportunity to do so. Do not *complain* about external circumstances such as an economic downturn, but plan, adapt, and persevere when challenges arise. Conditions that cannot be avoided must be *endured*, and it will do you *no* good whatsoever to whine and moan while you figure out how best to respond to states of affairs as they arise. Pay attention, make the best inferences you are able, and act so as to mitigate the suffering for yourself and for those in your care. It is irrational to become despondent because of events that you cannot control. Do

the best you can. Pay
attention.

May 13, 2021

The celebrities of your day become increasingly ludicrous and the vast majority of their behavior and utterances are clearly deleterious to society at large. Most of these people are imbeciles, liars, and moral reprobates, but the general public seems to offer them a degree of deference that indicates the masses either do not *realize* what kind of cultural disease they foster by treating celebrities as if they are superior to the general run of humanity, or they simply do not *care* about the various damages done by these miscreants. Perhaps it is the public, or at least that portion of it that pays special attention to the nonsense spouted by the celebrities, that ought to bear the brunt of the blame for these circumstances. Celebrity is, by its very nature, a parasitic existence. One can be a celebrity only to the extent that some portion of the public is willing to spend time and money attending to one's exploits, after all. If *you* simply *declare* yourself a "star," that declaration is more likely to be met with ridicule than with broad public approbation. The *masses* determine who qualifies as a "celebrity" and who does not. If *they* (the common, anonymous "they") decide to throw themselves at the feet of some narcissistic jackass, then they will gradually build precisely the culture that *they* deserve. As it happens, you are surrounded by the culture that *they* deserve. Does that mean that *you* deserve it as well? Perhaps you should not be too quick to answer that question. Where do *your* entertainment dollars go?

May 14, 2021

If the pervasive depravity and vapidity of life in the contemporary United States of America is *not* a *reductio ad absurdum* against the modern liberal "value" system and collectivist attempts at social engineering, then someone needs to buy a round of drinks for every adult in the nation. American "culture" is just one pathology piled on top of another until someone decides to start kicking down the things that are already falling from the weight of their own awkward stupidity. There is no doubt that some people are useless imbeciles, but this blindingly obvious fact must (apparently) *never* be pointed out, and it must certainly never serve as the basis for *any* policy, preference, or even any simple choice on the part of any individual to avoid unnecessary contact with the imbeciles. Everyone is encouraged to attend college, even though it is empirically demonstrable that not more than fifteen or twenty percent of the population possess the wherewithal to benefit from college-level instruction. The solution to problem, *obviously*, is to eviscerate academic standards to the point that *everyone* can pass their pointless courses and obtain a worthless diploma. What could be simpler? If standards are in place that exclude the masses, then the *standards* are *clearly* the problem. Did you hope to have access to a cardiothoracic surgeon who had dedicated a life to the project of becoming the very most highly-skilled and reliable physician possible and, moreover, one who has been endowed with natural intellectual excellence and preternaturally steady hands? How very *elitist* of you! If a ham-fisted middlebrow cannot

have the same opportunity to
perform surgery on your heart
as the most innately gifted
among us (supposing innate
gifts are not mere illusions
and fictions), then society
is better off without any
heart surgeons at all.
Egalitarianism demands that
we all lead equally
miserable, non-descript lives
of quiet acquiescence. Any
suggestion that some people
and some careers are "worth
more" to society at large
than are others can only be
attributable to some form of
indefensible *supremacy* or
other. The professional drug
addict and the neuroscientist
both explore functions of the
brain, do they not? Anyone
who dares suggest that one
deserves more praise than the
other must be made to *regret*
that suggestion.
Uncomfortable truths are not
to be treated as *truths*
anymore. Thus, a once great
nation passes into history.
It is to be replaced by a

bleating, undifferentiated herd of dumb animals. Take to the woods while you still can, and never return to this festering stewpot of iniquity and idiocy if you can help it. At least the *animals* can tell the difference between predators and prey.

May 15, 2021

Human beings untethered from their Creator or, at the very least, a *belief* that they have a Creator, are nothing more than primates with brains too large for the rest of them to manage. People who reject the concept of God are generally self-destructive, and they nearly always prove disastrous to those unfortunate enough to fall into orbit around the unbelievers. Mao, Stalin, and countless petty despots unrestrained by the supposition that they will, one day, face an unerring and unblinking Judge, have created nothing buy misery and oppression for those under their thumbs. To be sure, there have been, and there *are*, plenty of sincere believers who have made a hash of things under their control, and the Inquisition is hardly a shining example of humanity at its best, but it is always the *unbelievers* who adopt the project of constructing secular substitutes for God and religion, and it has always been the worship of the State and its minions that has generated the most pervasive wreckage and societal ruin. The Commandment to refrain from worshipping or "bowing down to" anyone and anything other than God is good advice whether God exists or not, and every time this counsel is flouted, the consequences are calamitous. The simple truth of the matter is that humankind cannot be trusted to avoid the worship of *itself* without the concept of a power to which *all* of it is subject. *Never* worship anything created by the talking primates. It is all just monkey business. Pledge your allegiance to the *source* of all worldly things, or pledge it to no one and nothing at all.

May 16, 2021

You continue to live and move among the humans, you continue to find their utterances and behaviors baffling, and you no longer remember when you began to experience members of your own species as something alien and incomprehensible, but *here* you are. *There* they are. More and more, you hope that "the twain" shall meet as infrequently as possible. What in the world are you supposed to say to someone who drones on endlessly about the travails of life in the American middle class? Perhaps you could point out that the American middle class has access to goods and luxuries that no monarch could have imagined just a century ago, or maybe you might note that this litany of challenges is being offered in an air-conditioned coffee shop where wireless Internet access is readily available, and no sign of starvation, slavery, or genocide is observable within even the most expansive conception of "driving distance." Lately, you have even caught *yourself* complaining about conditions for which half the population of the planet would voluntarily trade away limbs and internal organs. Are you, perhaps, becoming somewhat *too* human for your own liking? To *whine* is human, is it not? Cast your eyes to the night sky. With a little luck, a meteorite will come to the rescue with an impact properly describable as "extinction-level." In lieu of that, there is always the option of withdrawal from the company of others. Try to avoid uttering curses as you take your leave. You need not go away mad in order that you simply go away. Another alternative is learning to laugh at the disintegration

of your species. They had a
good run.

May 17, 2021

Many of the humans seem to panic when they encounter even the slightest *hint* of a minor risk. The massive and ever-increasing use of anxiolytic medications is not surprising, given the psychological and emotional fragility that appears to lie so close to the very *core* of most denizens of the contemporary world. The weakness on display is simply stunning. *How* do any of these pathetic weaklings make their way from one day to another? They *shriek* if they see a person not wearing a mask even at a distance of fifty feet or more, and they lose their minds if anyone uses a word to which they have some irrational aversion or other. You have witnessed these snowflakes dissolving in tears and hysteria because of the "misuse" of a *pronoun*. Anyone who cannot maintain sanity during an encounter with a syllable *cannot* possibly survive an *actual* assault or a *genuine* dose of adversity with composure or rationality intact. Presumably, the *over-reactors* are behaving disingenuously on most of the occasions in question, but *that* does *not* make you more confident about their psychological stability moving into the collective future of the nation and its culture. Anyone who feels compelled to *pretend* to be "offended" by someone else using one pronoun as opposed to another, clearly cannot be counted upon if and when genuine dangers arise. These people will *never* be assets. The simple solution is to have as little to do with the ultra-delicate types as is humanly possible. Treat them as if they are skunks. That seems particularly apt given the population in question.

May 18, 2021

How timorous are you prepared to become in your efforts to avoid offending hypersensitive, irrational weaklings? Paradoxical though it may seem, the dictatorship of the pathetic and useless seems to be the cultural default for the foreseeable future. You encounter "men" every day whom you would have backhanded on general principle just a few years ago, had they dared to demand obeisance to their moronic speech codes and childish claims of victimhood. At what point did the culture at large decide not only to *tolerate* these mice masquerading as men, but actually to *obey* their petulant commands as if they had been delivered upon tablets from Mount Sinai? In earlier, more rational times, these worthless creatures would have been beaten into submission and silence after *one* shrieking, peevish outburst. There *was* a time when these crybabies would have been raised in a home inhabited by their actual, biological fathers, and the *earliest* instances of this type of behavior would have been met with swift and severe punishment. Any father worth his salt would refuse to allow the shame of a carping, disrespectful son to sully the home he had worked so hard to provide. Alas, this culture has jettisoned *shame* in favor of utterly *unearned* self-esteem. Now, people who have accomplished less than nothing with their lives see fit to lecture the rest of us about how to conduct our affairs and, for some as yet undisclosed reason, no one breaks their bones or bludgeons them into unconsciousness. The ascendency of the wimps is a peculiar phenomenon indeed. When the strong learn to *fear* the weaklings, you can be sure that something has gone horribly wrong.

May 19, 2021

If you find that you have gotten off to a bad start in your day, then do something to serve as a countermeasure as soon as you realize that things are not going as you would have hoped. The countermeasure in question need not be anything dramatic or complicated (though it *can* be). Perhaps you would benefit from picking up a book that has served as a source of inspiration for you in the past, and reading a brief excerpt to get your cognitive train back on track. Some people find that their resolve is strengthened by reading passages from scripture. If you have a Bible nearby, you might read a few selections from *Proverbs* or *Psalms*. If you prefer the Quran, then one of the shorter *Surahs* might be sufficient to remind you of your devotion to a purposeful life. If scripture is not "your thing," then you might turn to the *Meditations* of Marcus Aurelius, the *Enchiridion* of Epictetus, or Tolstoy's *A Confession*. Lots of other sources of inspiration could be listed, but the point is made. Sometimes, you might be better off *listening* to an inspiring piece of music or a brief poem such as Rudyard Kipling's "If." Then again, you might just need one more cup of coffee, or twenty pushups to get the blood flowing, the mind cleared, or the bowels unblocked. Never underestimate the power of exercise to jumpstart a lackluster morning. Whatever you need, get to it expeditiously so that you can get back to the task at hand in a condition of optimal functioning. Get your head on straight, get to work, and move past moments of discouragement or lethargy. *Never* use such challenges as *excuses*.

May 20, 2021

The world will never run dry of idiots, charlatans, miscreants, or pathetic sloths. The supply of each type is regularly replenished, and the numbers are steadily on the increase. Do not despair merely because most of the people that you meet seem to be dimwitted, distracted, or utterly indifferent to the pursuits that you find most fascinating and most worthy of your greatest efforts. Not everyone cares a great deal for the pursuit of wisdom or virtue. The pursuit of wealth, fame, and bodily pleasure appears to be *far* more popular than any interest attaching to the goods of the mind. Why should you care what *other* people do with their limited time and energy? If they use up their resources in irrational fashion, then the consequences of doing so will serve as punishment enough for their poor decisions. Furthermore, why should you *want* other people to suffer because of their choices? Their suffering does not enhance *your* wellbeing, does it? *You* are *not* made healthier by your neighbor's *ill* health. You are *not* made wealthier by your neighbor's descent into poverty. You are *not* made wiser by your neighbor's dalliance with idiocy. You should either wish others well, or you dispense with concern for them one way or another. Though it is *tempting* to revel in a moron's travails, it is probably not particularly healthy or salutary to do so. Keep yourself on the narrow path of virtue. *That* is challenge enough. Let others stray as they please. Mind your *own* business and leave everyone else to live their lives as they see fit. No one appointed you *Guardian of the Multitude*.

May 21, 2021

Never lose sight of the fact that the world was here *long* before you showed up, and the implication that there were objective *facts* long before any human beings existed to notice them, uncover them, or theorize about the laws governing the natural world. You hear and read *so* much nonsense these days about how people "create their own reality," and advice to dimwits that they should "speak their truth," that you cannot help but wonder if the words "reality" and "truth" have lost all meaning for the people who say these kinds of things. Reality is the collection of all *facts*. Facts are conditions obtaining in the world *itself*, and they do not reside inside the heads, or the perceptions, or the beliefs of individuals or collectives. If everyone drops dead tomorrow, then all

of the same facts will still
obtain, with the exception of
the fact that there are lots
of living people. Jupiter
will still be the largest
planet in this solar system,
even when there is no one
around to call it "Jupiter"
or to notice its size.
Speaking *the* truth (you do
not get *your own*), is simply
a matter of expressing
propositions that correspond
to the objective facts "out
there" in the world *itself*.
If you state that the world
is a certain way, and it is,
in *fact* (in *itself*), the way
you have stated, then you
have stated the *truth*. We do
not get to *decide* what is and
is not true. We get to
attempt to *discover* what is
and is not true. Sometimes we
fail. Your *failure* to
understand reality is not
"your truth," any more than
your failure to win a
footrace is "your victory" in
that race. Try not to become

frustrated with idiots who speak gibberish.

May 22, 2021

It seems that the future is quite likely to *belong* to Islam. The West is (not so) gradually turning to Islam because of the gaping God-shaped vacuum left by the retreat of Christianity. Is there any particular reason to regard this incipient development as a misfortune or as something that you ought to *dread*? You have read the *Quran*, and you find *nothing* uniquely objectionable in its pages. Indeed, the clarity and confidence of its presentation are a welcome departure from the relativism, nihilism, and narcissism that currently dominate the cultural landscape across the West. The depravity and decadence of the contemporary Western world need to be replaced by *some* sustainable set of values if the total collapse of the West is to be avoided.

The Islamic worldview is, without question, preferable to and more ennobling than the worldview espoused in the halls of colleges and universities all over The United States, Western Europe, and Canada in the 21st Century. Any version of Shariah law has got to serve as a superior system of justice compared to the hypocrisy and duplicity currently practiced in courtrooms across the West, and promulgated by legislatures run by minions of corporations, trade unions, and special interests with deep pockets. Frankly, a bit of Islamic theocracy would be a welcome change from the vapidity and dishonesty of the political and cultural charade that poisons all human interactions wherever it holds sway. Imagine a world in which everyone was expected to work toward the fulfillment of Allah's commands, and in which anyone failing or refusing to honor the Creator of the cosmos is expected to pay a price for that failure in *this* lifetime, *and* in the wake of the *ultimate* dispensation of justice. What would the worst moral miscreants do in such a world? In the contemporary West, they control the levers of political and cultural power. The hands with which they perpetrate their crimes might get *cut off* in an Islamic State. That would *not* be the *worst* thing that ever happened, would it? Yes, you may well *hope* that the future belongs to Islam.

May 23, 2021

The life *without suffering* is *not* worth living. Consider the most important lessons you have ever learned, and ask yourself if you would have learned those lessons had you not suffered first. In most cases, particularly those cases involving the kinds of lessons without which your life would have been deprived of irreplaceable value, the pain was indispensable to the intellectual and emotional maturation that followed. It is simply not possible to be a real adult without having endured trauma and heartbreak along the way. People who have had the misfortune never to have endured *genuine misfortune* are condemned to remain children for the duration of their "charmed" lives. Would you *want* to inhabit a body devoid of scars? At your age, what excuse could you possibly conjure to explain the lack of damage? Clearly, it is much more fun to tell the stories of sustaining injury than it is to explain smooth muscles and unblemished skin. Look at the scars on your face, head, neck, abdomen, and knees, and realize how fortunate you have been to have experienced all of the pain, discomfort, and rehabilitation that attended those injuries. Imagine a life in which you had never felt a bone snap, or you had never heard a ligament pop. What a tragic existence that would have been. You have heard your own voice howling in agony, and you know what it is to have no idea if your body will ever work properly again. It is a pity that so many people cannot say the same. What can they really know about themselves? Wish them some healthy suffering.

May 24, 2021

They are the undead, they are the People of the Void, they are the masses who believe in absolutely *nothing*, and their representatives now control the levers of power in every significant institution across the entire Western world. Any hope that the West will come to its senses and step back from the brink of madness is obviously misplaced. When it comes to The United States of America in particular, any suggestion that the future is going to be anything other than dismal and disastrous is nothing more than an embarrassing attempt to deny a societal collapse that passed the point of no return a *long* time ago. This nation is very clearly *dying*. The bizarre stew of pathologies that is sometimes, in what can only be a misguided attempt at irony, described as a "culture," is an utterly indefensible concoction. When you wonder how in the world you and your fellow citizens have allowed this descent into degeneracy, perversity, and aimless nihilism, you seem always to make your way back to the taproot of all evil. It is *exactly* what it appears to be. The first words uttered by the serpent in Genesis are the words, "Did God really say," followed by a *lie* about what God really said. Whether God actually exists or not, a society that jettisons *belief* in God, or gives up on the notion of absolute, objective, universal moral facts, does so at its own peril. When you encounter the term "Godforsaken," remember that "forsaking" is sometimes a two-way street. Why should God *not* turn away from people who have turned away from Him? Human beings left up to their own devices *always* create a disaster of one type or another.

Remember that Stalin and Mao killed *many* more people than this Inquisition ever managed. When terrestrial rulers imagine themselves to be the final authorities, you can be certain that horrors will soon follow. Put as much distance as you can between you and the "culture" now surrounding you. The usual consequences are already spreading like tentacles of some dread beast.

May 25, 2021

Self-loathing is unhealthy for everyone, with the notable *exception* of morally vile people who engage in repugnant actions and have no inclination to regret or repent of the things that they continue to do. They *should* loathe themselves, but they do not. Make no mistake about the fact that there are many people on the face of this planet without whom the world would, quite clearly, be a better place (even if only slightly so). People who derive pleasure and satisfaction from causing other persons as much misery as they possibly can are neither fictitious nor, alas, particularly uncommon. You have met hundreds of people who clearly spent a *lot* of time and energy going out of their way to be annoying, irritating, and even sources of wretchedness to family, "friends," associates, and complete strangers. Consider all of the times you have felt compelled to ask questions such as, "*What* in the world are you doing?" or "What the hell is *wrong* with you?" only to be "answered" with a maniacal cackle or a non-ironic devilish grin. Poe wrote about "the imp of the perverse," and he was clearly writing about a genuine feature of the human condition. You sometimes experience the impulse to do the *wrong* thing precisely because it *is* the wrong thing. You have even given in to this impulse on the odd occasion, and you have experienced remorse in such cases. Some people do not seem to resist such impulses at all, and they seem not to regret the things they do under the influence of Poe's *imp*. Perhaps those people are, in some sense, more *honest* than you. What is the price of that type of honesty, though? You should *decline* to pay that price.

May 26, 2021

Pretending that a problem does *not* exist is a very *poor* strategy for solving that problem. Unfortunately, it is also a very *popular* strategy among members of the media, the professoriate, and the political sphere. The strategy is popular because there is a sense in which it *works*. It does not "work" in the sense that it alleviates anyone's suffering or in the sense that it reduces or staves off any danger (quite the opposite, in fact). It "works" in the sense that the public will keep consuming media that tell the people what they want to hear, students will flock to professors who do not challenge them to look objective and dispassionately at the facts staring them in the face, and the voters will continue to vote for politicians who spout optimism and reassuring nonsense. Of course, there will always be *some* appetite for prophecies of doom, but the majority of the masses will never admit that their nation is in decline, that their culture stumbles further into depravity by the hour, and that it becomes more obvious every day that the "optimists" are lying to the public. The masses will never admit to themselves that, in the final analysis, *they* are the problem. In a democracy the public gets the politicians for whom the majority votes, and the consumers get the goods, services, and media that are produced by the corporations receiving the lion's share of the commerce. Why are so many politicians so *obviously* corrupt? Well, it is *not* because a virtuous public insisted upon voting only for the "best and brightest" among their number. Why are the "values" exhibited in most movies, television shows, Internet broadcasts, and popular music so thoroughly perverse? Well, it is *not* because the public demands integrity and decency from its celebrities. The people *are* the root of all evil, but they comfort themselves by blaming the politicians for whom *they* vote, the corporations that *they* patronize, and the cultural icons to whom *they* pay unreflective obeisance. The public is mostly stupid, short-sighted, selfish, and devoid of any moral compass. The masses deserve *exactly* what they are getting. They will also deserve what comes next. What about *you*? If you deserve better than the others, then you should be able to provide *evidence* of your moral and intellectual superiority. Good luck with that. Perhaps you will realize what you *truly* deserve, but maybe you will come to this realization just a little too late. Time is *always* short, is it not?

May 27, 2021

The world is *full* of people, and *that* is *most* of the problem. The solution is, of course, fairly obvious, but it does not follow that anyone is actually going to *do* anything to solve this particular problem. This type of situation occurs on a regular basis. A blindingly obvious solution to a fairly significant problem goes begging for someone to do what is both necessary and evident, but no one is willing to do what clearly needs to be done. Consider the growing crisis involving tons upon tons of plastic ending up in the oceans. This is, to put the matter mildly, *not good*. Soon, it will be difficult to catch fish that have not ingested plastic detritus. Is there *really* any difficulty, however, in figuring out some way of reducing the amount of plastic waste that gets dumped in the oceans? *Stop making things out of plastic.* This simple step would guarantee that the problem will cease to be exacerbated, and it would facilitate efforts to clear the seas of plastic junk as much as the nations and corporations of the world can manage. So, when is this simple and obvious measure going to be enacted? As is so often the case, the thing that needs to be done will be accomplished too late or not at all. People have become so dependent upon this substance that did not exist for nearly *all* of human history, that they prefer ecological disaster to doing without plastic gadgets and packaging. Willful ignorance will prevent the clear solution from coming to fruition. Desire will trump reason. Indeed, the epitaph for the human race could well read, "Alas, desire trumped reason," and that expression could be emblazoned on the Moon as a warning to any species that may come to inhabit this planet in the future. Could not the same epitaph serve just as well on most *individual* tombstones? How often have *you* allowed desire to eclipse *your* reason? In the final analysis, it seems that the human beings just do not *want* to do what they know they *ought* to do. The exceptions to this rule are fairly few and very far between. Thus, humanity suffers needlessly. All available evidence indicates that they will do so until the very end. Prophets of doom have long declared that the end is nigh. Perhaps they have had it right all along.

May 28, 2021

It is a new day, and you find
that you have nothing new to
say. That sentence rhymes.
This is about as good a place
as any to stop. The end,
indeed, is nigh.

Printed in Great Britain
by Amazon